Pentecost 2

Proclamation 4

Aids for Interpreting
the Lessons of the Church Year

Pentecost 2

Susan R. Garrett
James H. Garrett

Series A

FORTRESS PRESS   MINNEAPOLIS

PROCLAMATION 4
Aids for Interpreting the Lessons of the Church Year
Series A: Pentecost 2

Library of Congress Cataloging-in-Publication Data
(Revised for vol. 5–7, ser. A)

Proclamation 4.

Consists of 24 volumes in 3 series designated A, B, and C, which correspond to the cycles of the three year lectionary. Each series contains 8 basic volumes with the following titles: [1] Advent-Christmas, [2] Epiphany, [3] Lent, [4] Holy Week, [5] Easter, [6] Pentecost 1, [7] Pentecost 2, and [8] Pentecost 3. In addition there are four volumes on the lesser festivals.
    By Christopher R. Seitz and others.
    Includes bibliographies.
    1. Bible—Liturgical lessons, English.   2. Bible—Homiletical use.   3. Bible—Criticism, interpretation, etc.
4. Common lectionary.   5. Church year.
I. Seitz, Christopher R.   II. Proclamation four.
BS391.2.S37   1989   264'.34   88-10982
ISBN 0-8006-4167-1 (Series A, Pentecost 2)

The paper used in this publication meets the minimum requirements of American National Standard for Information Sciences—Permanence of Paper for Printed Library Materials, ANSI Z329.48-1984.   ∞™

Manufactured in the U.S.A.   AF 1–4167

93   92   91   90   89   1   2   3   4   5   6   7   8   9   10

Contents

The Tenth Sunday after Pentecost

Lutheran	Roman Catholic	Episcopal	Common Lectionary
1 Kings 3:5–12	1 Kings 3:5, 7–12	1 Kings 3:5–12	Exod. 3:13–20
Rom. 8:28–30	Rom. 8:28–30	Rom. 8:26–34	Rom. 8:26–30
Matt. 13:44–52	Matt. 13:44–52	Matt. 13:31–33, 44–49a	Matt. 13:44–52

FIRST LESSON: 1 KINGS 3:5-12

Solomon's dream at Gibeon takes place early in the reign that he took over from his father David (1 Kings 2:10-12). David had charged Solomon to walk in God's ways in order that Solomon might prosper (2:1-4). Solomon got off to a good start in fulfilling this charge: He loved the Lord, and walked in the statutes of David his father (3:3). Solomon worshiped God at Gibeon (a prominent city and cultic center northwest of Jerusalem), offering up generous sacrifices there.

While at Gibeon, Solomon dreamed that God appeared to him and bade him to ask what gift God might bestow. Solomon had been ruling just long enough to know both the difficulties and the temptations entailed by the task. He could have requested that God grant to him still more of the power and the honor that went with being king. But Solomon recognized that the "perks" of his job were useless if he could not lead the people wisely! Hence he responded to God by recalling his father David's righteous conduct, as well as God's steadfast love for David, which had been demonstrated by the fulfillment in Solomon of God's earlier promise that one of David's descendants should sit upon Israel's throne (2 Sam. 7:12-16). In describing himself as "but a little child" placed by God to rule a great and numberless people (vv. 7-8), Solomon used hyperbole to express his humble awareness of the magnitude of the task confronting him. He then asked for the wisdom to govern the people justly, to "discern between good and evil" (v. 9). In other words, Solomon desired to procure not abstract wisdom nor wisdom for its own sake, but the practical wisdom necessary to carry out effective rule. God was so pleased with Solomon's prudent request that Solomon would be granted even more than he asked: He would be the wisest of all persons in all times (v. 12; cf. 4:29-34).

7

Moreover, God would grant also the things that Solomon had *not* requested: riches, honor, and length of days (3:13-14).

Modern Christians may think that they will never be faced with a moment of decision such as the one faced by Solomon. But in fact we make similar choices—choices about what is important to us in life—every day. We choose how we will spend our energy, our money, our time. Often our culture interferes with our ability to discern what are the right choices: We are bombarded from every side with the message that if only we know the right people, buy the right products, read the right magazines, or watch the right TV shows, our life will be enhanced. Given this situation it is very easy to lose sight of what is truly valuable in life. Solomon's commitment to service of God and his discernment of the need for God-given wisdom in order to carry out such service provide a worthy example for us to emulate.

ALTERNATIVE FIRST LESSON: EXODUS 3:13-20

This text presents the second segment of the story of the call of Moses (3:1—4:17). God had appeared to Moses in the burning bush at Mount Horeb (3:1-6), and had charged Moses to go to Pharaoh to bring forth the oppressed people of Israel (vv. 7-10). Moses, who had been rejected once before while trying to help his people (2:11-15), had protested first that he was unworthy of such a calling (cf. Isa. 6:5; Jer. 1:6; 1 Kings 3:7). God had answered Moses' objection by promising to be present with him. In the present lection, Moses proffers a second excuse: When he reports to the people that the God of their forebears had sent him, the people will demand to know God's name. (Verse 13 reflects one of two strands of tradition according to which God's name "Yahweh" was revealed first to Moses; cf. Exod. 6:3.) God's initial response to this objection, "I am who I am," or "I will be what I will be" (equally valid translations), utilizes a form of the verb "to be" (*'ehyeh*) which is related etymologically to God's name, Yahweh. The same form of the verb "to be" occurred only two verses earlier: God had said "I will be (*'ehyeh*) with you" (v. 12). Hence God's response to Moses' question suggests that God's character is disclosed by the divine presence in events past, present, and yet to come. On the other hand, there is a sense in which the response of v. 14a is a mysterious evasion: God's specific intentions will indeed be revealed in the future ("I will be what I will be"), but in sovereign freedom God refuses to disclose them now (cf. 33:19). In v. 15 (which stems from a different strand of tradition), God gives an alternate, more explicit answer to the Israelites' hypothetical question; this answer stresses the continuity of God's actions now with those done to the Israelites' own forebears. God next lays out the events which will follow upon Moses' address to the people. They shall request permission to depart, and will be allowed to do so—but only after God compels the Egyptians "with a mighty hand." Moses, who seems not to believe God's assurances of ultimate victory, proceeds to raise yet two more objections. These, however, lie outside the scope of the lection.

Homiletical application of the passage could take at least two courses. One approach would be to use the lection as a jumping-off point to consider the entire call of Moses (3:1—4:17), focusing on his remarkably stubborn resistance to God's will. Even when given every assurance of God's help and presence, Moses prefers to continue in his old state of alienation from his people. How often do we, as 20th-century Christians, prefer our comfortable old ways to God's challenging new ones, in matters both great and small? An alternate homiletical approach would be to focus more narrowly on vv. 13-20, exploring both the people's hypothetical question (Why would they want to know? Do they want to control God? Do they no longer trust God after their many years of oppression?), and the faithful constancy as well as the freedom of God that are exhibited by the response. The God "I AM" is the God who has promised to be with Moses. This is also the God who was with the Israelites' forebears, who has seen the people's affliction in Egypt, and who will accompany them on their way out of bondage. But at the same time, this is a God who cannot be controlled or manipulated by those who would seek to escape God's demands.

EPISTLE: ROMANS 8:26-30

The passage occurs as part of a lengthy excursus starting at Rom. 8:1-2 on "life in the Spirit." Verses 26-27 discuss the Spirit's intercession on behalf of believers, and vv. 28-30 discuss the beneficial purpose that is served by all events—even the experience of suffering—in the lives of Christians.

In the earlier part of chapter 8, Paul had explained that we who are believers participate in two realms at once: On the one hand, we are filled with the Holy Spirit, and so take part in the divine realm. On the other hand, while in this earthly life we take part in the human realm also, for our bodies are still subject to suffering, death, and decay. The source of our Christian hope is the divine promise that one day the spiritual realm will supplant the mortal, human one: God who raised Christ from the dead will give life to our mortal bodies through the Spirit, which dwells in us (Rom. 8:11). We wait with eager longing for that final day when our mortal bodies—and, indeed, when *all* of creation—will be set free from bondage to death and decay (vv. 19-25).

Paul begins the pericope by affirming that in the interim, while we are still subject to human suffering and limitations, our participation in the divine realm works to our great advantage. Though our feeble and rebellious human intellect cannot fully comprehend God's ways and cannot by itself enter into dialogue with the infinite God, the divine Spirit which is in us more than compensates for these shortcomings. By ourselves we do not know how to pray, but the Holy Spirit knows the mind of God perfectly (cf. 1 Cor. 2:11) and intercedes with God on our behalf. The expression translated by the RSV as "with sighs too deep for words" may originally have referred to the practice of glossolalia ("speaking in tongues"; cf. 1 Cor. 14:14-15); it may equally well be said to describe the experience of mute and prayerful awe before the Creator and Sustainer of life. In v. 27 Paul affirms that God, who "searches human hearts" (cf. 1 Cor. 4:5; 8:3; also Psalm 139; Acts 15:8; Heb. 4:12-13; Rev. 2:23), understands perfectly these prayers of intercession offered by the Spirit, because the Spirit intercedes in a godly way. Thus the Spirit bridges the chasm between the human and divine realms.

This first section (vv. 26-27) would be an excellent text for a sermon on prayer. Often we may feel as though our prayers go unheard; we may wonder whether we are, after all, talking only to ourselves. Paul assures us that such is not the case: The Holy Spirit hears our prayers and carries them to God. Or, we may feel that our prayers are inadequate because we cannot find the words to say what it is that we feel. But Paul tells us that the Spirit knows us better than we know ourselves, and reports our prayers to God in a language that God understands. The way to God is open and God waits to hear our supplications.

In v. 28 Paul shifts focus, resuming the discussion of Christian sufferings begun in v. 17. It is true, Paul implicitly acknowledges, that in this earthly life Christians undergo trials and tribulations. Paul does not say that God is the source of these sufferings but does affirm that God *uses* such sufferings for purposes that are ultimately beneficial to Christians, those who "love God" and are "called according to God's purpose." Whenever Christians suffer they are being "conformed to the image" of Christ, who also suffered (v. 29; cf. v. 17). Just as God brought Christ from death to life, so God will one day bring Christians from their existence of trials and sorrows to glorious new life (cf. Phil. 3:10-11). Christ is called "the first-born among many brethren" (v. 29) because the resurrection glory that he now possesses he will one day share with his Christian brothers and sisters.

The predestination language in vv. 28-30 functions not as an abstract reflection on the freedom of the human will, but as a pastoral assurance that the sufferings and distresses of the present age are not random or meaningless. On the contrary, Paul claims, such sufferings help to achieve God's eternal purpose, which is the redemption of humankind. Ever since long ago God has willed that believers, who are caused by circumstances to be conformed to the image of the suffering Christ, should also be conformed to the image of the glorified Christ. God has "justified" such persons (i.e., declared them to be righteous), and has bestowed on them the divine glory that will one day be made manifest to all (v. 30). To be sure, God's "glorifying" of those who are "called according to God's purpose" remains essentially a future event, to take place only at the judgment (cf. Rom. 5:2). But, on the other hand, it is quite right for Paul to speak of the glorification as already accomplished, inasmuch as Christ, whose image Christians take on, has already been glorified (cf. 2 Cor. 3:18), and inasmuch as Christians already possess the Spirit as a guarantee of the coming harvest of glory (Rom. 8:23).

The question "Why do good people suffer?" has nagged humanity at least since the time of Job. Paul does not answer the question "why," but he does offer assurance that God works through human suffering to achieve good. Life in the present age is subject to the reign of death and decay (see Rom. 8:18-25), but because of Christ's resurrection Christians know that the reign of death will one day give way to the reign of God. When they suffer Christians conform to the image of Christ, who also suffered; this conformity will be completed when God brings them, like Christ, from death to life in God's kingdom. God does not desire for creatures to suffer. But while they suffer, God assures them that the Spirit is with them and promises them that their hope of redemption will find fulfillment.

If using the Common Lectionary, the preacher could treat the lection from Romans in conjunction with the lection from Exodus (discussed above). Both passages convey the message that God is present with us. This assurance does not guarantee that the way ahead will be easy: At the time of his call, Moses still has much to suffer, and even after Christ's resurrection Christians are subject to death and decay. But God is present with us as with Moses and the Israelites and assures us that our redemption awaits us.

GOSPEL: MATTHEW 13:44-52

The lection includes four parables that are themselves part of a larger collection of Jesus' parables (13:1-52). The four under study are said to have been uttered to the disciples alone (13:36). Each teaches about a different aspect of the "kingdom of heaven." (Matthew's use of this phrase instead of "kingdom of God" is not exegetically significant; the phraseology indicates only that Matthew shared his Jewish contemporaries' pious reluctance to mention God's name.)

In the first parable (v. 44), the comparison of the kingdom of heaven to a hidden treasure echoes Prov. 2:4, which proclaims that wisdom and the understanding of God's words and commandments are to be sought "like silver," and searched for "as for hidden treasures." The "treasure" of the kingdom of heaven is of such surpassing worth that all other possessions pale in comparison. The man in the parable understands that by selling all he has and purchasing the treasure in a field, he has received the bargain of a lifetime!

When interpreting the parable's significance, the economic imagery is on the one hand not to be taken literally: One cannot "buy one's way" into the kingdom in the same way that one "buys" a field (cf. Acts 8:18-24). The parable's image of one selling "all that he has," on the other hand, should be taken seriously if not literally, inasmuch as it points to the radical nature of the commitment that the kingdom of heaven requires. This radical demand is illustrated more fully in Matthew's related story of Jesus' encounter with a rich young man, whom Jesus instructs to sell his possessions, give to the poor, and obtain "treasure in heaven" (19:16-22). The young man turns away "sorrowful," failing to perceive that the treasure spoken of by Jesus is priceless in comparison to earthly treasure (cf. 6:19-20). Had he perceived this truth, then he—like the man in the parable under study—would have been joyful and willing to commit himself unreservedly to the newfound "wealth."

The second parable, the story of the pearl of great value (vv. 45-46), is similar to the previous one. Here too, the focal points of the story are the surpassing worth of that which has been found, and the finder's willingness to commit all his resources in order to obtain it.

These first two of the four parables in the lection make essentially the same point and so could be treated together in the sermon. They deal with one particular choice in life: the choice to participate in the kingdom of God by being a follower of Christ. Jesus teaches that such participation is so very valuable that all other treasures pale in comparison. The day's first lection (1 Kings 3:5-12) could also be brought into the sermon: Like the characters in the first two parables, Solomon recognized that the treasures that God gives are of far greater value than monetary wealth or other "worldly" treasures. All three stories teach that the value of such God-given treasure is so inestimable that, in order to obtain it, one should be willing to give up things that the world holds dear.

In the third parable (vv. 47-50), the image of a fishing net that draws in fish of every kind is used as the basis for a teaching about the day of judgment. The parable resembles that of the tares and the wheat, which teaches that the "children of the kingdom" coexist with the "children of the evil one" (13:24-30, 36-43). More than the other evangelists Matthew stressed that Jesus proclaimed the inevitability of judgment and the corresponding imperative to live righteous lives (see esp. 25:31-46, only in Matthew). By carefully arranging and editing these judgment traditions Matthew emphasized that membership in the church would be no guarantee of salvation on the day of reckoning. For example, in the parable of the wedding feast Matthew has Jesus say that "both good and bad" are invited to the banquet (22:10; contrast Luke 14:23). But once assembled not all are judged worthy, "for many are called but few are chosen" (Matt. 22:11-14, only in Matthew; on this point see also Matt. 7:21-23; 13:24-30, 36-43). No doubt Jesus and Matthew assumed that the judgment would encompass all persons, inside and outside the church. But Matthew directs the parable, and the Gospel as a whole, to the believing community (insiders). In light of this focus, and in light of Matthew's insistence that church membership does not guarantee salvation, one can understand the fishnet that "gathers fish of every kind" in 13:47 to be symbolic of the church, which already by Matthew's day has in it both good persons and evil ones. The teaching that unfolds in vv. 48-50 then offers comfort to those genuinely righteous believers who see corruption and evil within the very bounds of the church; simultaneously the parable offers warning to those who misguidedly trust that their own claim to be disciples will save them, but who on the contrary will be told "I never knew you; depart from me, you evildoers" (7:23; cf. 25:46).

For Christians today (as in Matthew's day), the parable of the fishnet teaches that the business of judging between bad and good persons in the church is to be left to God. Jesus elsewhere told his disciples that he would make them fishers of human beings. The church, like the fisherman, is to cast its "net" wide. Followers of Christ are to be actively *calling persons into the church*. Inevitably, Matthew teaches, some who are unrighteous will be found even in the midst of the church. But this situation is not for Christians to correct. The "sorting out" is for God—and God alone—to do.

The fourth parable included in the lection (13:51-52) rounds off the block of parables that began at 13:1. The disciples answer "yes" when Jesus asks if they understand his teachings (contrast Mark 4:13). The Gospel was written to a postresurrection community, and one can imagine that the members of Matthew's church understood Jesus' question to be directed to themselves, who were also disciples: "Have *you* understood all that I have taught?" The word translated by the RSV as "has been trained" in Jesus' response to the disciples (Matt. 13:52) is a passive form of the verb *mathēteuō;* it is related to the word for "disciple" (*mathētēs*), which itself designates one who learns. Jesus is comparing the disciples, who "learn" the ways of God by understanding and obeying Jesus' words, to scribes who have learned the law of God, which Matthew reveres (5:17-20; see 23:34 for another favorable portrayal of scribes). Jesus' comparison of such disciples/scribes to "a householder who brings out of his treasure what is new and what is old" (Matt. 13:52) may refer to Jesus' own *new* interpretation of the *old* law (see 5:17-19, and note Jesus' ensuing reinterpretations of many of the ethical teachings set down in the law). Or, if Matthew has created the saying, it may apply to his and the church's own "new" appropriation of the "old" traditions of Jesus.

A sermon on these passages could be arranged in at least two ways. One way would be to give attention to the gospel's demand for unconditional commitment—symbolized in the first two parables by the characters' selling of all that they own in order to obtain the great treasure. The third parable could then be used to emphasize the serious nature of this demand: one's choices in life will have eternal consequences. Jesus himself stresses the solemnity of these matters, asking today's hearers of the gospel, "Have you understood all this?" A second approach to the lesson could focus especially on the third parable's implicit command to be about the business of "fishing for humans"—of calling them into God's church—and to leave the task of judgment to God.

The Eleventh Sunday after Pentecost

Lutheran	Roman Catholic	Episcopal	Common Lectionary
Isa. 55:1–5	Isa. 55:1–3	Neh. 9:16–20	Exod. 12:1–14
Rom. 8:35–39	Rom. 8:35, 37–39	Rom. 8:35–39	Rom. 8:31–39
Matt. 14:13–21	Matt. 14:13–21	Matt. 14:13–21	Matt. 14:13–21

FIRST LESSON: ISAIAH 55:1-5

Isaiah 55:1-13, the culmination of the prophecies of Second Isaiah, is a triumphant celebration of Israel's imminent return from exile. The first five verses call the reader to hearken to the prophet's message of hope and salvation (see esp. v.3). The call echoes the invitations to Wisdom's banquet in Prov. 9:3-6, 11 and in Sir. 24:19-22. The use of images associated with nourishment suggests that attending to the prophet's words—the Word of the Lord—will bring life abundant. Note that a similar metaphor is used later in the chapter, when the prophet compares his words to the rains sent from heaven, which cause life to grow and prosper (vv. 10-11).

Isa. 55:3b-5 transfers God's promise to David of an everlasting covenant (2 Sam. 7:4-17) to the entire people of Israel. Note especially the way that v. 5 echoes Ps. 18:43-45, but applies the saying to Israel instead of to David alone. The assurance that God's promises stand would have been welcomed by the Israelites, who were experiencing the anguish not only of exile from their homeland, but also of believing that God had betrayed them (see esp. Ps. 89:38-51). In response to such anguish the prophet assures the people that God is faithful (cf. Jer. 33:19-26). But the promise to David is now reinterpreted: It is no longer David whose victories shall "witness to the people" (i.e., testify that the Lord is on Israel's side). Rather, God will so glorify the whole people (v. 5) that *they* shall be such a witness. Distant and foreign peoples will want to join themselves to the people of Israel because of the manifest way that God supports the chosen nation (cf. Isa. 44:5; 45:20-25; and note that Isa. 55:6-9 is treated below).

In times of trouble, it is easy to begin to think that God is against us. The sufferer may regard the ordeal as a punishment for sin, or as a sign that God has betrayed him or her. It is in such times of feeling alienated from God that we are most tempted to give up our faith commitment. We

ask ourselves, Why should we continue to be obedient when God seems
not to care about what happens to us? The Israelites, exiled to Babylon,
apparently felt this way (see Psalm 89). To them the prophet proclaims
that God has not abandoned them! Even in their moment of sorrow, when
they feel that hope has been lost, God invites them to come to the holy
banquet, to listen to God, and to feast upon God's life-giving Word. And
God assures them that the covenant relationship endures. So also in our
own moments of greatest anguish God is near, saying "Incline your ear,
and come to me; hear, that your soul may live" (Isa. 55:3).

ALTERNATIVE FIRST LESSON: EXODUS 12:1-14

A sermon on this lection, treated in conjunction with the lection from
Matthew (discussed below), could reflect on the nature of those acts of
corporate worship when we remember what God has done for us. Such a
sermon would be a natural lead-in to celebration of the Eucharist.

The account of the institution of the Passover festival reflects a long
period of development of oral tradition and liturgical practice. Literary
critical study of the account, and comparison of the Passover story with
similar cultic traditions from the ancient Near East, suggest that the festival
had an independent origin, apart from the Exodus material. The Passover
probably originated as a rite of semi-nomads who wished to ensure protection against the dangers of an annual spring migration from desert to
cultivated land. As the biblical author has presented it, however, the story
of how the Hebrews were spared from the death of the first-born has been
tightly woven into the Exodus story: The death is the straw that finally
breaks down Pharaoh's stubbornness (12:29-32). Pharaoh and the Egyptians
suffer a devastating loss, and the people of Israel depart, not waiting even
long enough for their dough to be leavened (vv. 33-34). (Of course the
Hebrews' hasty exit is still not the end of the story; in 14:8 Pharaoh will
once again "harden his heart," when the people arrive at the Red Sea
[Hebrew: sea of reeds]).

In 12:14 the Lord tells Moses to institute a festival that shall be celebrated
in perpetuity to commemorate these significant events. The Passover celebration is to be followed by the seven-day festival of unleavened bread.
If taken too literally the sequence is confusing, since vv. 15-19 presuppose
a household setting, which is not consistent with the unfolding events (the
people are in the midst of flight from Egypt). The confusing sequence has
resulted from the dual function of the passage: It is both a historical account
and a liturgical manual reflecting centuries of vicarious participation by

the Jews in the described events. As Professor Brevard Childs comments, the integration of the past and the future in this passage points to Israel's status as "a people who has been redeemed, but who still awaits its redemption" (*The Book of Exodus* [Philadelphia: Westminster Press, 1974], p. 205).

In subsequent generations, even up until the present day, the Jewish people have joined together as a worshiping community at Passover to remember God's act of deliverance. From a very early date the Passover shaped the Jews' hope of future redemption by God. For example, according to some Rabbinic traditions the Passover night was to be kept as a "night of watching" (Exod. 12:42) because it was the night when God traditionally saved the righteous; it was thought also by some to have been Passover night when Shadrach, Meshach, and Abednego were saved from the fiery furnace and when Daniel was saved from the lion's den. The remembrance of Passover shaped early Christian hopes as well: Some scholars have argued that the belief in Passover night as the night of redemption influenced the early Christian conviction that the Lord would come at night (see, e.g., Mark 13:33ff.; Rom. 13:11; 1 Thess. 5:1ff; Rev. 3:3; 16:15). In celebrating the Passover, Jews (and early Christians) looked to the past and perceived there the sure foundation for future hope.

EPISTLE: ROMANS 8:31-39

By asking in v. 31, "What, then, shall we say about these things?" Paul cues the reader that he is about to give the final word in his discussion of Christian suffering, begun in 8:17 and most recently continued in vv.28-30 (discussed above). Moreover, the theme "God is on our side," which resonates through 8:31-39, is a fitting climax to the entire discussion since 3:21.

Paul launches his summation with the first of several rhetorical questions: "If God is for us, who is against us?" The question echoes such Old Testament passages as Ps. 23:4; 56:9, 11; and 118:6-7, in which the psalmist proclaims absolute trust in God's presence and support. The "if" of v. 31b does not imply uncertainty; one could translate "*inasmuch as* God is for us . . .", since Paul has in vv. 29-30 given strong testimony that God is, indeed, on our side. In v. 32 Paul states an additional reason for such confidence: So much does God love us that *even God's own son* was not spared. The wording recalls Gen. 22:16: Abraham loved God so much that he would not spare even Isaac, his beloved son. But whereas God had at the last moment intervened to prevent Isaac's death, no such intervention had prevented the death of Jesus. God's choice not to spare Jesus was proof of God's amazing love for humankind (Rom. 5:8). Paul reasons that if God loved us enough to give Jesus up to death, then of course God will give us all other things, since no gift could be as costly to God as the one already given! The nonspecific "all things" probably refers to those things that are necessary for salvation (cf. Rom. 5:10).

Next Paul assures his readers that with God and Christ as allies they need not fear that they will be accused and condemned at the judgment. Since it is God who justifies Christians, who would possibly condemn them? (vv. 33b-34; the precise punctuation varies from one translation to the next, and the ancient manuscripts have no punctuation at all). The question echoes Isa. 50:8-9, in which the prophet declares his confidence that because God stands with him, no adversary can successfully contend with him or find him guilty. Since God is the judge, the "defendants"—who have already been justified by that same God (Rom. 8:30)—will necessarily prevail. Condemnation is out of the question! This truth is made doubly sure because Christians have none other than Christ Jesus, who died and was raised to God's right hand, as their advocate before God (v. 34; cf. v. 26; also Heb. 7:25 and 1 John 2:1).

But can anything separate Christians from Christ's love? Can tribulation, or distress, or persecution, or famine, or nakedness, or peril, or sword (v. 35)? Paul's quotation in v. 36 of Ps. 44:23 (and see Psalm 44 in its entirety) ups the ante on the question, giving voice to a concern that may well have been on his first readers' minds: "If our new commitment to Christ is, in truth, the way to be faithful to God, then why does God allow us to suffer? Perhaps God has abandoned us." Quite possibly those first readers wondered whether their experience of suffering indicated that God was angry about their newfound commitment to Christianity, regarded as the "lunatic fringe" of its time. By addressing this fear head-on, Paul robs it of its virulence and also provides a foil for his lyrical conclusion in vv. 37-39.

In v. 37 Paul begins his final assurance by stating a paradox: Far from indicating God's displeasure, the hardships that the faithful undergo actually demonstrate *victory over evil!* Those who suffer with Christ will be glorified with him. The verse echoes Paul's earlier statement that all things work together for the good of those who love God (v. 27; see the discussion of the previous lection). The word in v. 37 that is translated by the RSV as "more than conquerors" is an emphatic form of a word frequently used to describe the "conquering" or "overcoming" of evil (as in, e.g., Rom. 12:21; Luke 11:22; Rev. 12:11). The poetic chain ensuing in vv. 38-39 encompasses all of the created world: there is *nothing,* nothing anywhere in the universe, that could ever separate us from the love of God which has been manifested in our Lord, Jesus Christ.

GOSPEL: MATTHEW 14:13-21

Matthew takes the story of the feeding of five thousand over from Mark (Mark 6:32-44; cf. Matt. 15:32-39 and 2 Kings 4:42-44), but alters it in several ways. First, Matthew strengthens the link between the feeding miracle and the preceding story of Herod's execution of John the Baptist. The report of John's death was the cause of Jesus' withdrawal to a lonely place. Matthew gives no insight into Jesus' psychological motivation (grief? fear for his own life?). But inasmuch as the execution of John foreshadows Jesus' own death, the editorial alteration serves to strengthen the eucharistic undertones of the miracle.

By noting that Jesus healed the sick among the assembled throng, Matthew adds emphasis to Mark's notice that Jesus had "compassion" on the people. Though Jesus sought to be alone, when faced with human need he responded with compassion. "Compassion" will also be the motive for Jesus' subsequent feeding of the four thousand (15:32), and is mentioned in connection with his healing activity (20:34; translated "in pity" by the RSV).

Matthew abbreviates the disciples' interaction with Jesus, causing them to appear more compliant (cf. Mark 6:37b). Matthew also makes the disciples' role in the distribution of the loaves more explicit (compare Mark's "in order that they might distribute [the loaves]" with Matthew's "and the disciples [distributed the loaves] to the crowds"). This highlighted role would have provided a model for the members of Matthew's community, who sought to emulate the disciples' behavior in feeding the hungry physically and spiritually (cf. Matt. 25:35); the model is equally valuable for Christians today.

Matthew omits mention of the distribution of the fish. As a consequence the story foreshadows the Eucharist even more strongly than did Mark's account (note the parallel sequence of verbs in Matt. 14:19 and 26:26; also in Mark 6:41 and 14:22: "Jesus took . . . blessed . . . broke . . . and gave . . ."). These eucharistic undertones are most fully developed in the Gospel of John—which, ironically, has no account of the Eucharist itself. In the Gospel of John the feeding story prompts Jesus to reflect that he himself is "the bread which has come down from heaven" (John 6:1-14, 26-40). Though Matthew reports nothing similar, it is probable that members of his community understood the story of the miraculous feeding as a preview of the Last Supper and also of their own eucharistic practice, when they themselves ate the bread of life.

There is a parallel to this story in Matt. 15:32-39, the feeding of four thousand (cf. Mark 8:1-10). Some commentators give the explanation that the second feeding story prefigures the participation of the Gentiles in the church, whereas the earlier feeding of five thousand symbolizes the participation of the Jews. There is, however, little grounding in the text for this view. It is more probable that Matthew (like Mark) is reflecting tradition, which knew of two separate feeding miracles (or perhaps of two versions of one event). The preservation of the two accounts by both Matthew and Mark is a measure of the importance of the feeding stories in the early church.

In the story of the feeding of the five thousand, Matthew recalls a miracle of Jesus in such a way as to evoke thoughts of the worshiping community's own regular celebration of the Last Supper. The notice preceding the miracle story, about John's death, prefigures the Lord's own impending execution. Jesus stands amidst the people as a suffering Lord, as one whose own body would soon be broken on the people's behalf. The language used to describe the miracle ("Jesus took . . . blessed . . . broke . . . and gave . . .") would have reminded Matthew's early readers that whenever they celebrated the Eucharist, they too were partaking of the bread of life. In doing so they remembered the Lord's life on earth, how he had compassion on his people and satisfied their needs. They would have understood Jesus' words, "You give them something to eat" (v. 16), as instructions not only to the Twelve but to themselves. As the disciples had fed hungry persons, so too did the members of the postresurrection community offer "bread"—the very bread of life—to those who "hungered for righteousness" (Matt. 5:6).

The preacher should help his or her listeners to appreciate that this story is not just an uncomplicated account of a miraculous deed, but a profound narrative that operates at several levels. First, it depicts an event in Jesus' earthly ministry. Second, it points ahead to the Last Supper and to Jesus' own death. Third, it foreshadows the situation of the church, whose members look eagerly to the day when Jesus will eat bread with them new in God's kingdom (Matt. 26:29)—and who, in the meantime, are instructed to feed a spiritually starving world.

The Twelfth Sunday after Pentecost

Lutheran	Roman Catholic	Episcopal	Common Lectionary
1 Kings 19:9–18	1 Kings 19:9a, 11–13a	Jon. 2:1–9	Exod. 14:19–31
Rom. 9:1–5	Rom. 9:1–5	Rom. 9:1–5	Rom. 9:1–5
Matt. 14:22–33	Matt. 14:22–33	Matt. 14:22–33	Matt. 14:22–33

FIRST LESSON: 1 KINGS 19:9-18

To make sense of the lection it is important to understand the sequence of events leading up to this scene (1 Kings 17:1—19:8). Elijah had been a staunch opponent of King Ahab and Queen Jezebel. Ahab held Elijah personally responsible for a drought that Elijah had predicted, and that (in fulfillment of Elijah's word) had long afflicted the land. Elijah's opposition to the rulers Ahab and Jezebel had reached its climax on Mount Carmel, where Elijah had defeated the prophets of Baal (supported by the ruling couple) in a dramatic contest to prove the reliability and power of their respective gods. Elijah, being "zealous" for the Lord, had subsequently slain the prophets of Baal (18:40; 19:10). Now Jezebel seeks Elijah's life (19:1-3, 10), and so he has fled through Judah and beyond Beersheba into the desert.

The scene described in this lection takes place in a cave on Mount Horeb, after Elijah's escape. The setting on Mount Horeb recalls Moses' reception of divine revelation at the same location (called "Sinai" according to the Southern [Judahite] tradition). In prayer with the Lord, Elijah bemoans his precarious and lonely position (vv. 9-10). It may be that the biblical author thinks that Elijah is complaining unjustifiably; after all, he is not in truth the *only* one who supports the Lord; cf. 18:39. Next God is revealed to Elijah. Especially after the experience on Mount Carmel, Elijah—and the reader of the narrative—might well expect the dramatic occurrences of earthquake, wind, or fire to be the medium for such revelation. But, on the contrary, only in the "still small voice" coming after these events does Elijah recognize the presence of God. Today also we desire to hear a word from the Lord. We may look for a dramatic sign from God, an indication that God is indeed present in our life. In our case, too, it may be that the Lord is not to be found in the earthquake, wind, or fire, but in the "still small voice." This "voice" may be the inner assurance that comes through prayer; a word of exhortation in a sermon, Scripture passage, or hymn; a word spoken by a friend. But we can be confident that God is speaking to us, if only we stop to listen.

Instead of directly comforting Elijah in his moment of anguish, the Lord commissions him to do more work (vv. 15-17). It is as if God is saying, "Stop worrying about yourself and worry instead about my work." In this regard Elijah's experience is similar to that of an earlier prophet who had found himself on Mount Horeb: Moses, too, had protested the Lord's plan to use him for taxing and dangerous work. Like Elijah in the present lection, Moses' objections were countered by the Lord's firm resolve (Exod. 3:1— 4:17). It may be that when we, like Elijah, pause to listen to the "still small voice," we will hear God telling us to worry about the Lord's work instead of about our own fears.

It should perhaps be noted that the overall structure of 1 Kings 19:9-18 is somewhat confusing. Verses 9b-10 seem to be repeated in vv. 13b-14; moreover, in v. 11a Elijah is commanded to stand outside the cave, but in v. 13 he is still in the cave. It may be that v. 9b-10 was a later addition to the narrative. In any case, the general sequence of events is clear enough, and their meaning is not significantly affected by the repetition.

ALTERNATIVE FIRST LESSON: EXODUS 14:19-31

The death of the Egyptians' first-born and the Hebrews' flight from Egypt were not the final events in the ongoing saga of God's providential rescue of the children of Israel from their oppressors. When they reach the Red Sea (Hebrew: sea of reeds), Pharaoh's heart is hardened yet a final time (14:4, 5, 8). Thinking that the Hebrews have lost their way (14:3), and regretting the decimation of his labor force, Pharaoh decides to pursue them to the sea. The biblical writer insists that all of these events happen in accordance with God's plan. Far from being "lost," the Hebrews have the Lord as their guide (13:18). Pharaoh is but an instrument to carry out God's plan; the defeat of the Egyptian ruler will serve to manifest God's sovereignty to the Egyptians (14:4).

When their prospects look the most grim, the people lose faith in Moses' wisdom (vv. 10-12). Suddenly the security of their former servitude looks more attractive than their present freedom, which is fraught with risks. Moses assures them that the Lord "will fight for them" (v. 14). The subsequent account of the Hebrews' crossing of the sea and of the drowning of the Egyptians fulfills this promise; the Egyptians themselves recognize before their demise that "the Lord fights for them against the Egyptians" (v. 25). The miraculous drowning convinces Israel that God is indeed on their side, and that Moses is truly the Lord's servant. But their repudiation of Moses' leadership at the height of the crisis foreshadowed the mistrust that will characterize their attitude toward Moses throughout the wilderness wanderings.

The preacher could treat this passage in conjunction with the passage from Matthew (Matt. 14:22-33; discussed below).

EPISTLE: ROMANS 9:1-5

The passage begins Paul's explanation of the place of the Jews in God's plan of salvation for humankind. Paul recognizes that the validity of his life's work and message depends on his being able to demonstrate that God has not forsaken the unconverted Jews. For, if God has forsaken the nation of Israel, to whom the covenants had been given and the divine promises made, then one would have to conclude that God has been fickle. In that case the assurances given at the end of chapter 8 would be meaningless; God might one day abandon the Christians also! Because Paul recognizes that his argument is vulnerable at this point, his tone becomes insistent, even defensive.

In v. 3 Paul gives voice to a strange wish: that he himself be accursed and cut off from Christ for the sake of the Israelites, his brothers and sisters, compatriots according to the flesh (the last phrase is meant to distinguish them from the Christians, many of whom were former Gentiles, and so "adopted" brothers and sisters). The tense Paul uses here (translated by the RSV as "I could wish") conveys hedging or uncertainty, as if Paul knows that such a wish could never come to pass but chooses to express it nonetheless.

Paul's wish is not unprecedented. His words echo the prayer of Moses, who prayed that he might be blotted out of God's book in order to restore the rebellious Hebrews to fellowship with God (Exod. 32:32). And Paul elsewhere states that Jesus had become accursed by hanging on a tree, in order to redeem us from the curse of the law (Gal. 3:13). Still, Paul's willingness even to entertain the notion that he himself be cut off from Christ for the sake of the Israelites reveals the depth and intensity of the apostle's feelings on this matter.

The rest of the passage elaborates the privileged position of the Jews (Paul had made a similar point, but in briefer form, back in Rom. 3:1-4). Paul says that the Jews are the chosen people of God, God's children, the ones to whom the covenants and the law have been entrusted, the ones who have been instructed on how properly to worship God, the ones to whom the promises of land, kingdom, and resurrection have been made. Paul does not say that any of these conditions has been nullified. On the contrary, he assumes that God *must* remain faithful and true to everything promised or given to the Jewish people. As Paul reasons elsewhere, "What if some Jews were unfaithful? Does their faithlessness nullify the faithfulness of God? By no means! Let God be true though every human be false" (Rom. 3:3-4a). Paul will expend considerable effort in the next few chapters explaining how God can and will remain true in the face of the Jews' present unbelief.

The preacher may want to use the text as the basis for a sermon on the special position of the Jews—a position, Paul insists, which will ultimately be upheld by God (see the exegetical discussion below of Rom. 11:13-15, 29-32). Or, using the text as a jumping-off point to consider the rest of Romans 9, the preacher may wish to reflect on the sovereignty of God, who is always ultimately faithful to promises made in the past, but who brings about their fulfillment in astonishing ways. Preachers who take the latter approach may choose to tie in the Common Lectionary reading from Exodus, which has a similar theme.

GOSPEL: MATTHEW 14:22-33

In Matthew's Gospel the account of Jesus' walking on the water has been transformed from a misunderstood manifestation of Jesus' deity (Mark 6:45-52) to a parable for the church in times of storm and trouble. The story is highly reminiscent of Matthew's earlier account of Jesus' calming of the storm: as in the previous incident, the boat is "beaten by waves" (14:24; cf. 8:23-27), a disciple cries out, "Lord, save me!" (14:30; cf. 8:25), and Jesus remonstrates him for his "little faith" (14:31; cf. 8:26). Matthew's introduction of the earlier account by noting that the disciples "followed Jesus" (8:23; contrast Mark 4:36, and note the content of Matt. 8:18-22), and the disciples' address of Jesus with the prayerful but distressed "Save, Lord" (8:25), indicate that Matthew interpreted that first incident as foreshadowing the risen Lord's calming of the stormy waters encountered in discipleship. There the disciples had been left wondering, "What sort of man is this?" (8:27). Now the story of Jesus walking on the water in chap. 14 serves to answer that earlier question.

When Jesus comes to the disciples on the water, they are understandably frightened, and he comforts them with the lordly "I am" (RSV: "it is I"; see Exod. 3:14, discussed above, and consult the commentaries on John

8:58). Here, just as at the transfiguration, Jesus reveals a glimpse of the divine glory that he will have after the resurrection.

In place of Mark's account of the disciples' utter failure to comprehend (Mark 6:51-52), Matthew has introduced an account of Peter's attempt to imitate Jesus' walking on the water (Matt. 14:28-33). Here as elsewhere, Peter should probably be viewed as representative of the disciples. Peter's request that Jesus bid him to join Jesus on the water is not impetuous or overconfident, as is sometimes asserted; rather, it is symbolic of a believer's entirely appropriate desire to emulate the Lord. Note that Jesus responds, not by reprimanding Peter, but by doing just what he asks: Jesus bids him, "Come." But Peter begins to sink and cries out "Lord, save me." Jesus' rescue of Peter foreshadows his rescue and strengthening of those who call upon his name in the postresurrection period. The chiding of Peter for his "little faith" is typical of Matthew; the words *oligopistos* and *oligopistia* (meaning "[having] little faith") occur in Matt. 6:30; 8:26; 14:31; 16:8; and 17:20 (elsewhere only in Luke 12:28). Matthew wishes to instruct his church that inadequate faith is their problem, just as it was Peter's problem when he tried to walk on water (see especially Matt. 17:20, and contrast Mark 9:29 and Luke 9:43).

When Jesus climbs into the boat, the wind ceases and the disciples "worship" Jesus, saying, "Truly you are the Son of God." The difference from the response of the disciples as portrayed by Mark (Mark 6:52) is striking. In general Matthew softens Mark's harsh portrait of the disciples, but something additional is going on here: Matthew is teaching his readers that it is in times of trouble, when believers call upon Jesus to save them, that the Lord is truly known.

A sermon built around this passage could focus on the theme of God's presence with the believing community in their efforts to live as imitators of Christ. The church today is called to follow Jesus into what may look like impossible situations; indeed, the community of faith is required to do nothing less than walk on water! (The preacher could elaborate with references to challenges facing his or her particular congregation.) Jesus bids us, as he bid Peter, to come. But like Peter, our faith is usually inadequate to the task. We find ourselves buffeted by the waves of uncertainty, of difficulty, of controversy. Matthew instructs us that it is precisely in such moments when the believing community must turn to Christ for salvation, being confident that he will reach out his hand to keep us from sinking under the waves.

The passage could be treated in conjunction with either the lection from 1 Kings, or (if one is using the Common Lectionary) the lection from

Exodus. Elijah's efforts to follow the Lord's commands had led him, too, into a seemingly hopeless situation; the Lord then appeared to him and gave him, not words of pity and reassurance, but a commission to new action. The Israelites had been following God's directions in their departure from Egypt, but at the border of the Red Sea ("sea of reeds") it looked as though all hope were lost. Precisely in this moment God intervened to save them. Christians today are called by God to enter into difficult situations. The way may be fraught with peril, but believers may be confident that God is with them, strengthening them, supporting them.

The Thirteenth Sunday after Pentecost

Lutheran	Roman Catholic	Episcopal	Common Lectionary
Isa. 56:1, 6–8	Isa. 56:1, 6–7	Isa. 56:1, 6–7	Exod. 16:2–15
Rom. 11:13–15, 29–32	Rom. 11:13–15, 29–32	Rom. 11:13–15, 29–32	Rom. 11:13–16, 29–32
Matt. 15:21–28	Matt. 15:21–28	Matt. 15:21–28	Matt. 15:21–28

FIRST LESSON: ISAIAH 56:1, 6-8

Chapter 56 of Isaiah begins the section often designated by scholars as "Third Isaiah." The consensus view is that the oracles included in Third Isaiah were composed after the people had returned from Babylonian exile to the land of Israel (probably between 530 and 510 B.C., and thus contemporary with Haggai and Zechariah). At this time the people were confronting the day-to-day realities of life in the restored community.

Verse 1 of the present lection is a call to righteousness, elaborated in v. 2 (skipped over by the lectionary) as specifically a call to obey the Sabbath. Keeping the Sabbath was one of the most visible indications that a person had made a decision to support Yahweh and the worshiping community; faithful Sabbath observance was increasingly urged upon the people in the postexilic period (cf. Isa. 58:13-14; Jer. 17:19-27).

Verse 3 proclaims that eunuchs and foreigners, who would have been considered outcast by this community (see Deuteronomy 23), need not fear that they are to be rejected by the Lord, or cursed because they have no children to carry on their name. Verses 4-7 elaborate the point, taking up first the case of eunuchs (vv. 4-5), and then that of foreigners (vv. 6-7). (These words of comfort to faithful eunuchs and foreigners anticipate in a very specific and concrete way the more general assurance in 56:8 of God's care for the "outcast"; hence, skipping over vv. 3-5, as does the lectionary, detracts from the force of v. 8.) "Isaiah" assures readers that the eunuch, who would have no offspring to carry on his name (considered to be a terrible situation; cf. Gen. 15:2), will in fact have a memorial that is "better than sons and daughters" (vv. 4-5). And, perhaps in response to a trend toward exclusiveness in postexilic Israel (exhibited by Ezra and Nehemiah), the prophet proclaims that foreigners faithful to Judaism will present sacrifices that are acceptable to the Lord.

It is easy to be an open and inclusive community in principle. But the prophet did not permit his readers the comfort of abstraction; for the community returning to the land, eunuchs and foreigners were perceived as offensive and undesirable. Indeed many would have supposed that such persons were unacceptable even *to God*. But the prophet insists that it is precisely these undesirable persons who will be included in God's kingdom. The modern preacher could draw an analogy to persons perceived as undesirable by his or her own congregation: It is just such persons whom God invites and blesses. This message concerning the inclusiveness of the divinely ordained community is also at the heart of the lection from Romans for this Sunday.

ALTERNATIVE FIRST LESSON: EXODUS 16:2-15

It is now the middle of the second month since the departure of the children of Israel from Egypt. They begin to "murmur"—to grumble in dissatisfaction—against Moses and Aaron, complaining that they would have been better off dead. One cannot determine from the text whether or not there was any factual basis for their anxiety that they would die of hunger (v. 3; contrast the more explicit 15:22 and 17:1). The biblical author, however, regarded their complaint as illegitimate: The unflattering words "to murmur" and "murmuring" are used repeatedly in 16:1-8. In telling Moses and Aaron that "you have brought us out" into the wilderness, the people conveniently overlooked the providence of God, who has been the force behind Moses' leadership (cf. Exod. 14:31, discussed above). Moses recognizes the people's murmuring for what it truly is: rebellion against the Lord (v. 8; cf. Neh. 9:17).

Initially it is not clear whether God's promise to rain bread from heaven is a direct response to the people's complaints or made on the basis of God's own initiative. Even if the former, the end of v. 4 indicates that God will use the gift of bread for other purposes, to "test" or "prove" the people's faith (the "test" could refer to events described either in vv. 19-20 or in vv. 27-29). But when Moses reports the Lord's words to the people, he claims that the Lord has indeed made the promise of bread in response to the people's murmurings. God then reiterates this point in the epiphany described in vv. 11-12. Even though the people are petty and undeserving— even though they complain against the very God who led them out of bondage—God will graciously satisfy their desires, in order that they might know that it is Yahweh their God who acts (v. 12). God is gracious, slow to anger and abounding in steadfast love and faithfulness (Exod. 34:6). In 16:13-14 the narrator reports the gifts of quails and manna (the latter word is said to be related to the Hebrew expression "what is it?"). The people of Israel would continue to eat the manna till they came into the promised land (v. 35), though the quail is apparently regarded as a onetime gift (note that according to Num. 11:4-6, 31-32, the quail only came later, when the people tired of manna).

The biblical text already reflects different perspectives on the meaning of the depicted events. The preacher could build a sermon around any of these several strands. According to one perspective, Israel's crying for bread indicated their stubbornness and ingratitude to the God who had led them out of bondage (vv. 6-8), while God's gift of bread from heaven exhibited the deity's graciousness even when spurned. The Israelites thought they were complaining only about food, but Moses identified the true nature of their complaint: They were rejecting the lordship of Yahweh. Understood thus, the story is a paradigm for understanding God's relationship with Israel—and with the church—down through the ages. All day long God has spread out God's hands to a rebellious people (Isa. 65:1-7; Rom. 10:21).

According to another perspective discernible in the tradition, the gift of manna is a test by God of the people's obedience to the command to honor the Sabbath. God informs the people that sufficient bread will be given on the sixth day to make collection on the seventh day unnecessary; indeed, no bread will be given on the seventh (this line of thought is developed in vv. 22-30).

According to yet a third perspective discernible within the tradition, the gift of manna is a test of the people's willingness to trust God's grace (v. 4). If they try to gather more than the day's share, they will show themselves unwilling to rely on the providence of God. So also we who pray that the Lord "give us this day our daily bread" are challenged to remember that we do not own the future; we can look ahead and plan and be prudent stewards, but ultimately our lives are in God's hands. Therefore we must "let the day's own trouble be sufficient for the day" (cf. Matt. 6:25-34).

EPISTLE: ROMANS 11:13-15, 29-32

In last week's lection (Rom. 9:1-5), Paul expressed dismay over the failure of the majority of Jews to believe the gospel message. That exclamation introduced a lengthy effort by Paul to show that God has not reneged on the promises made to the Jews, despite their resistance to the gospel. In chaps. 9–11 Paul argues that, in showing grace to the Gentiles while permitting the Jews to remain in their unbelief, God is following a pattern established in the past: Now, as many times before, God is choosing who will be shown mercy and who will experience a hardening of heart (9:6-18). God, like the potter, elects to save one pot and to destroy another. But this "purpose of election" (9:11) does not imply that God is wantonly destructive. Just as the potter, having destroyed a defective pot, then creatively reshapes it (cf. Jer. 18:3-6), so also God will use the present disobedience of Israel to bring about the ultimate reconciliation of all, Jews and Gentiles alike.

According to Paul's unfolding argument, God has temporarily allowed the Israelites to disbelieve, in order that room might be made for the Gentiles. During this period of Israel's disbelief, the Gentiles will be embraced as God's own people (9:25-26). But at some future point God will reintegrate back into the people of God those Jews who are now estranged because of their rejection of Christ. Thus unrepentant Israel is like a natural olive branch that God has broken off so that a new, wild olive branch (the Gentiles) might be grafted in (11:17). Israel's role is also somewhat analogous to the role of Christ. God had not spared Jesus, but had willingly given him up, in order that through his death sinners might be reconciled to God. Similarly now God does not spare Israel, but willingly permits some of its members to be alienated from God, in order that through this alienation Gentiles might be enabled to take their place (promised in Scripture, Paul insists) among the people of God. Moreover, just as God had rescued Christ from death, so also Israel will eventually be rescued from its state of disobedience. The natural olive branch—broken off to make room for the wild olive branch—will be grafted back into the tree (11:23).

In 11:1 Paul states explicitly the question that has been driving the whole argument: Has God rejected the chosen people? No. Rather, God has elected a remnant (the Christian Jews) who, because of God's grace, have been faithful. All the rest of Israel has been hardened (11:7-9). But this "stumbling" by the majority of Israel will not cause the unbelievers finally to "fall." When they see that their own rejection of Jesus has been the very occasion for God's mercy toward the Gentiles, they will become jealous, and so will seek reconciliation with God. In the given lection, Paul claims that he "magnifies his own ministry" in order to fan the embers of this life-saving jealousy among his unbelieving Jewish brothers and sisters (11:14).

God has deemed that the present unbelief of the majority of Jews should make possible the inclusion of the Gentiles in the people of God. In other words, by temporarily "hardening" the Jews, God has brought about the reconciliation of the world. How much greater, Paul reasons in vv. 12-15, will be the benefit conferred by the eventual return of the Jews to the fold! The acceptance of the Jews back into the people of God will mean nothing short of "life from the dead." The yearning of all creation—to be set free from the bondage to decay, and to achieve the freedom of the glory of God's own children (8:21)—will at last be realized. To conclude his argument Paul reiterates that the gifts to Israel (mentioned in 9:4ff) and call to be God's chosen people have not been revoked (v. 29). Just as the Gentiles once were unfaithful but now have been shown mercy and so believe, so also the disbelieving Jews will finally be recipients of mercy. God's promises are unshakeable; God's desire to be reconciled to the world knows no bounds and stops at no obstacle. Paul's insistence that God has not forsaken the Jews, but will one day "graft them back" in to the people of God, has significance for the church today. The gentile portion of the church—which certainly includes the vast majority of modern Christians— has no right to boast or to condemn the Jewish people, for the Gentiles owe their own inclusion in the church to Israel. Israel is like Christ, who was not spared. What a humbling insight! And, as Christ was raised to new life, so the people of Israel shall be reincorporated into God's people. The preacher should perhaps note that the question of Israel's fate is not necessarily tied to the political fate of the modern nation of Israel. Paul insists that God acts in God's own time and in God's own way; humans cannot by their feeble machinations force God's hand.

Understanding the text in more generic terms, one could preach about the inclusiveness of the kingdom of God, not only with regard to Gentiles and Jews but also with regard to other marginal peoples—peoples whom the establishment church may prefer to forget. This is also the message of the texts from Isaiah (discussed above) and Matthew (discussed below).

GOSPEL: MATTHEW 15:21–28

The story of the Canaanite woman's faith provides an interesting counterpoint to last week's lection from Matthew. In that incident Jesus had chided Peter for his "little faith," which kept him from being able to walk on the water. The implication was that had Peter's faith been greater, he would not have begun to sink. Here we have an altogether different sort of story, which nonetheless shares as background the theme of the power deriving from persistent faith. The woman's remarkable faith is able to overcome the barrier separating Gentiles from the God of the Jews.

In taking over the story from Mark, Matthew has emphasized Jesus' separatism from the gentile woman. Whereas in Mark's account Jesus had from the start interacted with the woman directly, in Matthew's version the initial interactions are mediated by the disciples. Although for her part the woman does address Jesus ("Have mercy on me, O Lord, Son of David!"), the narrator tells us that "he did not answer her a word" (only in Matthew). After the disciples complain to Jesus that the woman is a nuisance, Jesus responds that he was "sent only to the lost sheep of the house of Israel" (also only in Matthew). Thus the narrative reflects the view that during his earthly life Jesus restricted the scope of his mission, preaching to and serving the Jewish people only. The sole Gentiles to whom he ministered were the centurion whose servant was ill (8:5-13), the Gadarene demoniacs (8:28-34), and the woman in this story.

The disciples' complaint to Jesus that "she is crying after us" heightens the impression of urgency and of the woman's conviction that Jesus can, indeed, help. She calls him "Lord, Son of David"—an address that is all the more striking because the one who utters it is not herself a Jew and so cannot have been expected to appreciate the messianic title (see 2 Sam. 7:12-16, understood by some first-century Jews as a prophecy of the coming Messiah). Her persistence is astonishing: Even when Jesus says that he will not help her, she kneels before him and addresses him as "Lord" (vv. 24-25). And when Jesus utters the biting phrase that compares Gentiles to "dogs," rather than cringing with fear or offense the woman retorts in kind: "Yes, Lord, yet even the dogs eat the crumbs that fall from their masters' table." Jesus is impressed by the woman's remarkable display of confidence in his ability to heal her daughter. He proclaims, " 'O woman, great is your faith! Be it done for you as you desire.' And her daughter was healed instantly." Jesus' response recalls his earlier acclaim for the faith of the gentile centurion (8:10).

The present episode is one of several pieces of evidence that Matthew's community included Jewish Christians who were dealing with tensions created by the assimilation of Gentiles into the church. The question of whether and how to carry out such assimilation was an enormously difficult problem in the earliest church; it is reflected, for example, in the selection from Romans included in the lesson for the day (discussed above), and also in Acts 15. To those who would resist such assimilation, Matthew proclaims, not that the different roles occupied by Jews and Gentiles in God's plan for salvation no longer exist, but that God rewards faith wherever it is found. Matthew will, moreover, emphasize that although the earthly Jesus went only "to the lost sheep of the house of Israel," after his resurrection the Lord commissioned his followers to "make disciples of all nations" (28:19).

Early readers of Matthew's Gospel may have seen their own image reflected in the depiction of Jesus during this encounter with the Canaanite woman. They, like Jesus, were at first reluctant to acknowledge the insistent clamoring of outsiders who wanted to experience Christ's presence and power. Jesus had relented, as if to say that the old barriers must give way in the face of such remarkable persistence and faith as the woman had shown. Matthew's readers would have realized that they must likewise extend the gospel to those whom they had previously excluded.

The problem of Gentiles' entry into the church is long past. The preacher will want to point out, however, that today's community of faith faces similar challenges. All around us we see men, women, and children who are crying to hear the gospel—but they are not always the sorts of persons we are accustomed to having in the pew beside us. Are we willing, as Christ was, to respond to their entreaties? Are we prepared to acknowledge that they, too, have the right to eat at the master's table? Are we able to recognize that their faith in Jesus may be as great—or greater—than our own? These are the questions Matthew's first readers must have asked themselves; in today's world, the characters have changed but the questions remain the same.

The Fourteenth Sunday after Pentecost

Lutheran	Roman Catholic	Episcopal	Common Lectionary
Exod. 6:2–8	Isa. 22:19–23	Isa. 51:1–6	Exod. 17:1–7
Rom. 11:33–36	Rom. 11:33–36	Rom. 11:33–36	Rom. 11:33–36
Matt. 16:13–20	Matt. 16:13–20	Matt. 16:13–20	Matt. 16:13–20

FIRST LESSON: EXODUS 6:2-8

At God's direction, Moses and Aaron had gone to Pharaoh, requesting permission for the people of Israel to take a three-day journey into the wilderness to worship the Lord (5:1-3). But Pharaoh's response had been disheartening, to say the least: rather than granting the request, he had ordered the Egyptian taskmasters to increase the Hebrews' workload. The children of Israel were to make the same number of bricks as before, but were required to gather the needed straw themselves (5:4-19). Hence the people had expressed great resentment of Aaron and Moses for asking Pharaoh to let them depart (5:20-21). Moses had cried to the Lord, and the Lord had assured him, saying "with a strong hand Pharaoh will send them out" (5:22—6:1). In the present lection (6:2-8), God continues the address to Moses with a self-disclosure, and with reassurance that the "groaning" of the people of Israel has been heard and the covenant sworn to Abraham (Genesis 17) not forgotten. The people will yet be redeemed from their bondage and brought into the land sworn to Abraham. God will accomplish this "with an outstretched arm and with great judgment"—in other words, with actions that demonstrate in no uncertain terms the Lord's sovereignty even over Pharaoh.

Thus the present lection, which may have originated as part of a parallel account by the Priestly writer to God's self-revelation on Mount Sinai (Exodus 3), constitutes God's answer to Moses' complaint of 5:23. The answer takes the form, not of a justification for what has happened thus far, but of the Lord's fresh self-revelation. God assures Moses that the promises made to the patriarchs long ago would not be forgotten: God is not whimsical or unreliable in dealing with the children of Israel. In the present narrative context—after Pharaoh has not only denied the Hebrews' request, but has even exacerbated their plight—Yahweh's assurance seems somewhat puzzling. But the answer points to the mysteries of God's divine workings in history, which from the human perspective may at times seem paradoxical or even illogical. Early readers of the text knew what the narrative character Moses could not: that God would indeed redeem the people with mighty acts of judgment and "make good" on the promise to Abraham. However dark the moment might have looked to Moses and the Hebrews, history would reveal the wisdom and trustworthiness of God's plan.

ALTERNATIVE FIRST LESSON: EXODUS 17:1-7

Once again the people find fault with Moses and, in his words, "put the Lord to the test." In contrast to the episode preceding God's initiation of the daily gift of manna (see the treatment of Exod. 16:2-15 above), in this instance the biblical author concedes that there was a genuine physical need: "there was no water for the people to drink." The strength of the people's complaint is indicated by Moses' fear that they will stone him (v. 4). The Lord again answers the need of the moment, causing water to flow forth from a rock that Moses strikes (cf. the closely parallel incident at Num. 20:2-13). The reference to "the rod with which you struck the Nile" (Exod. 17:5) subtly recalls God's earlier signs and wonders, which had caused Pharaoh to allow the people of Israel to depart. The evocation of that earlier deliverance helps to make the point that despite God's continuing care for them, exhibited in one astounding sign after another, the people are utterly lacking in trust, either of God or God's servant Moses. In remembrance of this faithlessness, the place where the water came from the rock was named "Massah" and "Meribah," the Hebrew words for "proof" (because the people of Israel put God to the proof) and "contention" (because they were contentious).

The modern reader should not infer from the story that one can never complain to God about one's situation—the psalms of lament demonstrate that such complaint was a well-established tradition in Israel. But in such psalms, the believer's relationship with God is preserved, however deep the lament (see, e.g., Psalm 22). In the present lection, by contrast, the Israelites bemoan God's having led them out of Egypt (v. 3), thereby repudiating their former acceptance of Yahweh as Lord. Analogy might be drawn to complaints made within the context of human relationships: Such complaints can be made constructively, or they can be done in such a way as to sever the relationship entirely. In our relationship with God, the former is acceptable to God; the latter is not.

EPISTLE: ROMANS 11:33-36

Paul has just spent three chapters explaining a paradox: God has not abandoned the Jewish people but will use their present disobedience and estrangement as an opportunity for grace (see the discussions above of Rom. 9:1-5 and 11:13-15, 29-32). To Paul's readers it must have looked as though God was either fickle (having abandoned the Jews) or powerless (being unable to bring them to faith in Christ). But Paul has argued that neither perception is accurate. Rather, it is the case that the present disobedience of all but a remnant of the Jews is part of God's remarkable plan to bring about the obedience and reconciliation of all humankind. By God's mercy the formerly excluded Gentiles have been engrafted into God's people; by mercy the disobedient Jews also will be reconciled to God. The lesson for today celebrates the God who would go to such startling lengths to achieve reconciliation with rebellious humankind. Thus the doxology of vv. 33-36 serves as climax and conclusion to all of chapters 9–11.

In v. 33 Paul exclaims that God's judgments are unsearchable and God's ways inscrutable. The divine plan is too complex, too much a reflection of God's own infinite wisdom and insight, ever to be fully understood by finite humans. The exclamation is underscored by Paul's subsequent allusions (in vv. 34-35) to Isa. 40:13 (LXX) and Job 41:11. In each of these Old Testament passages, God's sovereignty and infinity are contrasted with human frailty and limitations. God's ways, including the divine plan according to which both Gentiles and Jews will finally be reconciled to God, cannot be discerned or understood by means of the finite human intellect.

But if God's ways are unknowable, how, then, has Paul understood the "divine purpose of election?" If pressed on this question Paul probably would have answered that he has understood because he is himself filled with the divine Spirit. This Spirit does indeed search and know the mind of God. Paul says as much in another letter, when he describes the divine "mystery" which is made known to the spiritually mature (1 Cor. 2:6-13). But in the context of Romans 11, emphasis is less on the means by which God's ways are comprehended, and more on the utterly astounding character of those ways. Who would have thought that God would refuse to spare God's only Son, but give him up to death in order that human slavery to sin might be ended? Who would have thought that God would refuse to spare the chosen people Israel, but give them over to disobedience in order that Gentiles, too, might find a place in the people of God? Who would have thought that death would give way to life? Or that disobedience will one day give way to faith and reconciliation? The scope of God's plan, the breadth and length of God's vision, are too much for the human mind ever fully to grasp.

The first lesson (Exod. 6:2-8) and this epistle lesson (Rom. 11:33-36) could be treated together in a sermon. The self-revelation of God in Exodus and the praise of God offered by Paul in Romans would provide an excellent foundation for a sermon on the character of God as sovereign, wise, and faithful. God's authority or sovereignty far exceeds that of Pharaoh. God's wisdom and knowledge far outstrip that of Moses. And God is utterly reliable with regard to the promises made to Abraham, Isaac, and Jacob. In Romans, Paul, too, recognizes God's sovereignty, wisdom, and fidelity. Paul has said that God is like a potter who exercises complete control over the clay. That sovereignty is exhibited now in God's decision to consign the Jews to temporary disobedience, that the Gentiles may be let in. Such an action by God seems both foolish and fickle from the human perspective, but Paul knows that the scope of God's foresight far outreaches that of humans. And one day it will be seen by all that God is completely reliable and true.

GOSPEL: MATTHEW 16:13-20

At Caesarea Philippi for the first time Jesus' disciples recognize him to be the Christ (Greek for "the anointed one," equivalent to "Messiah" in Hebrew). They have already acclaimed him as the "Son of God" (14:33). The present incident is initiated by Jesus; in the question of v. 13 the title "Son of Humanity" is to be understood as an alternate way of saying "I" (cf. Mark 8:27). The disciples inform him that the people are saying that he is John the Baptist (cf. Matt. 14:2); or Elijah, who was expected to accompany the advent of the reign of God (cf. 17:10-11; Mal. 4:5-6); or perhaps Jeremiah or one of the prophets. It is not easy to account for all these suggestions (especially the last) in terms of first-century beliefs, but the point is that people understand Jesus to be someone quite extraordinary. Nevertheless, they are not on the right track. In truth they have no idea who Jesus really is. On the other hand, Peter (here as elsewhere in Matthew the representative of the disciples) gives the right answer to Jesus' query: "You are the Christ, the Son of the living God." Jesus' response is strong and positive (contrast Mark 8:27-30). In Matthew's account Jesus blesses Peter and asserts that this knowledge has been divinely revealed. Thus the expressed opinions of the people and of Peter illustrate Matthew's conviction that the Christ, the Son of God, is known only by persons who have been granted spiritual insight; meanwhile the world remains in ignorance (11:25-27; cf. 1 Cor. 1:21-25).

Included in Jesus' blessing on Peter is the formal granting of a new name, *Petros,* which (in a play on words) Jesus pairs with the very similar word *petra,* rock. Peter is the "rock" upon whom Jesus will build his "church." Only here and in 18:17 in the canonical Gospels does the word church (*ekklesia*) ever appear on Jesus' own lips. This paucity of references, together with the great divergence of Matthew's account from that of Mark (Mark 8:27-30), have led many scholars to doubt whether Jesus actually uttered these statements. Interpreters who doubt the authenticity of the passage argue that it was created in the postresurrection period (perhaps by Matthew himself), when the tradition was well-attested that Peter had been one of the first to see the risen Lord (1 Cor. 15:5; Luke 24:34), and when it was widely known that Peter had become the chief apostle. Luke and John both indicate that after the resurrection Peter would be the one, as Luke put it, to "strengthen the brethren" (Luke 22:32; John 21:15-17). Whether or not the Matthean tradition is authentic to Jesus, it is clear that Matthew regards Peter's role in the emerging young church as a major one. Jesus declares that the church that Peter will help to govern will be as firm and enduring as a rock, so that even "the powers of death" (literally: the gates of Hades) will not be able to undermine it.

Jesus delegates to Peter "the keys of the kingdom of heaven," so that whatever decisions he makes on earth will be binding also in heaven. Though it is not clear in what sphere this authority is meant to be applicable, comparison with Matt. 18:18 and John 20:23 suggests that matters of discipline and forgiveness are at stake. The parallel passages are addressed to the disciples as a whole; it may be that in Matt. 16:19 Peter is once again functioning as representative of the larger group, so that the authority is delegated not to him alone but to all the disciples (as well as to those who exercise authority in imitation of them ever since).

In v. 20, taken over from Mark, Jesus commands the disciples not to tell anyone of his identity. Even if the disciples should try to make that identity known, the people would not understand; indeed, apart from Jesus' death and resurrection, they *cannot* understand who he is (cf. 17:9). Even Peter himself does not fully comprehend the implications of Jesus' identity as the Christ, as the next pericope from Matthew (considered below) clearly demonstrates.

A sermon on this passage could highlight the contrast between the accurate perception of Jesus' identity by his disciples and the inaccurate perception by those outside the movement. Today, as in Jesus' own lifetime, the world thinks that it knows who or what Jesus is, but in truth it does not. It is only those who have committed themselves to following Jesus who have eyes to see him as the Christ of God. At Peter's acclamation of Jesus, the Lord declares that Peter shall be the foundation of the church, with authority to issue discipline that is binding in the eyes of God. The preacher may choose to understand Peter's role here as representative of the disciples as a whole. Discipleship brings special privileges, including the gift of eyes to see what others cannot see. But the body of Christ is also entrusted with enormous responsibilities and must take these responsibilities with the utmost seriousness.

The Fifteenth Sunday after Pentecost

Lutheran	Roman Catholic	Episcopal	Common Lectionary
Jer. 15:15–21	Jer. 20:7–9	Jer. 15:15–21	Exod. 19:1–9
Rom. 12:1–8	Rom. 12:1–2	Rom. 12:1–8	Rom. 12:1–13
Matt. 16:21–26	Matt. 16:21–27	Matt. 16:21–27	Matt. 16:21–28

FIRST LESSON: JEREMIAH 15:15-21

This passage is one Jeremiah's five laments about his own role as doomsayer to a resistant people (cf. 11:18—12:6; 17:14-18; 18:18-23; 20:7-18). The laments all have a personal dimension; at the same time, they are often expressed in the stereotyped language of the lament such as is found in some of the psalms and in other prayers of lamentation.

This particular lament begins with Jeremiah's plea that God vindicate him by punishing those who oppose him. Jeremiah then reminds God that he, Jeremiah, has been obedient to God, and that it is on account of the prophet's unflinching faithfulness that he suffers. He has "eaten" God's words and taken delight in them, harsh though they are (cf. Ezek. 2:8b—3:3; Rev. 10:8-11). Moreover, on account of his acceptance of the commission to proclaim God's word, Jeremiah has endured isolation and unceasing pain (15:17-18). This pain is made the more acute by his conviction that it is undeserved. Has God abandoned the prophet? Is God no more reliable than a brook that dries up overnight (v. 18b)? In response, God reassures Jeremiah that the prophet will not be abandoned if he continues to do God's will. This is not to say that the way will be any smoother: The people will continue to fight against Jeremiah. But ultimately God will save and deliver the prophet.

The biblical tradition affirms that prophets who genuinely spoke God's message suffered for their testimony (see, e.g., Neh. 9:26). The early Christians understood Jesus as the greatest of the prophets who stood in this noble but tragic tradition (see, e.g., Luke 6:22-23; 7:16; 13:34). In modern history also, examples abound of persons who have suffered or died because they spoke the truth to a stubborn people. Christians today need to be reminded that the authentic word from God is not always a pleasant and comforting one; as Christ says to the church in Laodicea, "Those whom I love I reprove and chasten" (Rev. 3:19; cf. Prov. 3:12). Therefore persons who speak God's reproving word can anticipate that often they, like Jeremiah, will not be greeted with open arms. Certainly care must be taken, lest the tradition about the suffering of the prophets be used as an easy means to deflect criticism that is in fact well-deserved. But, provided that it is not treated casually, this lesson and others like it offer firm assurance that God is, indeed, with those who speak a prophetic word—even when it seems that God has departed, or that words fall on deaf ears.

ALTERNATIVE FIRST LESSON: EXODUS 19:1-9

This passage describes the preparation of the people to receive Yahweh's covenant (the entire account of the giving of the covenant extends through 24:11). Exodus 19:1 marks a decisive break with the preceding narrative, hinting that something momentous is about to occur. Verses 3-8 follow a traditional pattern for covenant renewal (cf. Josh. 24:2-28; 1 Sam. 12:1-25): God's deeds are proclaimed, the conditions of the covenant are given, and the people make a response of commitment. If Israel will remain faithful to God's covenant, then the people will have a special relationship with the Lord: They will be the Lord's own possession, a kingdom of priests, and a holy nation. The people respond with one voice that they will do what the Lord requests. The assent may seem to be problematic at this point, since no specific commands have yet been put forth. The people's expression of commitment is understood to have been made in anticipation of the particular requirements to be enumerated in the subsequent narrative. The implications of God's will have yet to unfold, but in principle the people are willing and ready. Verses 9-13 reflect Moses' special role as the divinely appointed mediator between God and the people. Moses is to go to the people and tell them to prepare themselves for God's appearance to them three days hence. The account of that appearance, and of the giving of the Ten Commandments, are covered in the subsequent two lections from Exodus.

EPISTLE: ROMANS 12:1-13

Romans 12:1 begins a new, hortatory section of the letter, but the inferential "therefore" in the first phrase of v. 1 indicates that Paul regards the ensuing exhortations as integrally related to the theological exposition of chaps. 1–11. The astonishing plan of God to show mercy to all ought to evoke a response of gratitude from believers—a gratitude so profound that its only adequate expression is the believers' uncompromised commitment of themselves to God.

In exhorting his readers to "present their bodies as a living sacrifice," Paul uses technical terms of sacrificial procedure. The ritual slaughter of animals as sacrifices to the deity (or deities) would have been familiar to both Jewish and Gentile readers, but Paul claims that the "sacrifice" that will be pleasing to God is the "metaphorical sacrifice" (RSV: "spiritual worship") that is performed by those who act out their faith commitment in the arena of everyday life. By analogy, in the church today, believers' commitment to living the Christian life on a day-to-day basis is the gift or "sacrifice" that is most pleasing to God.

Before commencing in v. 3 with specific instructions on how to carry out "spiritual worship," Paul includes another general exhortation (v. 2): Christians are not to be *conformed* to this age (RSV: "world"), which as Paul states elsewhere is "evil" and "passing away" (Gal. 1:4; cf. Rom. 8:18-25; 2 Cor. 4:16-18). Rather, Christians are to be *transformed* by the renewal of their inner beings. This renewal is effected by the Spirit, which is the guarantee that as Christians we will share fully in the age to come. As we are transformed by the Spirit to be ever more like Christ (cf. 2 Cor. 3:18), we shall be better able to "discern" or "approve" what is God's "good and acceptable and perfect" will (cf. Phil. 1:9-11).

The exhortation not to think more highly of oneself than one ought (v. 3) is especially appropriate in view of Paul's earlier warnings against arrogance. In the context of Romans, this warning was made to the Jews, who might boast of their relation to God because they have been instructed in the law (2:17-18), and to the Gentiles, who might erroneously think that they are better than the unrepentant Jews (11:17-20). Paul cautions that both groups ought not to "become proud," but to "stand in awe" (11:20). Such an admonition would have helped to counteract the tendency toward factions inherent in a mixed church such as the one at Rome. The advice is also needed in the church today. The unity and effectiveness of the church continue to be threatened by arrogance and spiritual pride—if not against members within a single congregation, then against congregations or denominations who "do things differently than we do."

Paul next borrows some of the advice first formulated in his correspondence to the Corinthians (vv. 4-8; cf. 1 Cor. 12:4-31). There the image of the church as "one body with many members" had been brought to bear on Christians who quarreled over the relative merits of different spiritual gifts. There is no evidence that the Roman Christians had similar disagreements, but Paul assumes that advice forged in the heat of the earlier controversy was applicable also to new situations. Paul puts before the Romans the ideal of a community working in harmony, using their respective talents for the upbuilding of the whole.

The lection concludes with a string of short but specific instructions meant to aid the Romans in their efforts to live out their "spiritual sacrifice" (vv. 9-13). The relevance of these instructions, which in the Greek consist almost entirely of a single long, rhythmic chain of participles, has not diminished in twenty centuries.

GOSPEL: MATTHEW 16:21-28

The passage follows Peter's pronouncement at Caesarea Philippi that Jesus was the Christ (16:13-20, discussed above). In v. 21 Matthew notes that "from that time" Jesus began to teach the disciples that he must suffer; in other words, he now begins to teach them the implications of the identity just perceived. There will indeed be dire implications, not only for himself (v. 21), but for his followers also (vv. 24-28).

Here Jesus predicts for the first time that he will suffer and be killed (cf. 20:18-19; 26:2). In 16:22b Matthew fills out Mark's account, giving the content of Peter's "rebuke" of Jesus. "God forbid, Lord!" Peter exclaimed (literally his words are "merciful to you," with "may God be" or "may heaven be" implied). Peter's horror is perfectly understandable. Prior to Jesus' death there was no expectation among Jews that the Messiah would suffer; indeed, most would have regarded the notion as preposterous. Such Old Testament passages as Isaiah 53, interpreted christologically by Jesus' followers, had not been interpreted in this way prior to Jesus' ministry. As Luke so eloquently narrates, it is only after the resurrection that the minds of Jesus' followers were "opened" to understand the Scriptures, "that the Christ should suffer and on the third day rise from the dead" (Luke 24:45). The message of "the crucified Messiah" would continue to be "a stumbling block to Jews," and "folly to the Gentiles" (1 Cor. 1:23).

Jesus, however, does not excuse Peter's words as understandable. Instead he interprets them as a manifestation of Satan's presence. Peter is a *skandalon,* a cause for stumbling (weakly translated by the RSV as "hindrance"). As during Jesus' time in the wilderness, Satan now seeks to prevent Jesus from fulfilling his God-given mission. Peter inadvertently serves as Satan's tool in this effort. There is a wordplay involved: Simon *Petros* (similar to *petra,* the Greek word for "rock" or "stone"; see Matt. 16:18) has now become the *petra skandalou,* the "stone of stumbling" mentioned in Isa. 8:14-15 and applied elsewhere to Christ (see Rom. 9:32-33; 1 Pet. 2:6-8). Jesus, the "stone of stumbling" for would-be followers, finds that for himself the "stone of stumbling" is none other than his own disciple! By being such a "hindrance," Peter shows that he is not of a mind with God (Matt. 16:23c). He is limited by his human notions of what the Messiah must be and do.

Next Jesus teaches his disciples the implications of his messiahship for them. Jesus instructs them that if they want to "come after him"—to be his disciples—then they must deny themselves and take up their crosses and follow him. The reference to the "cross" at this point suggests that the way of the disciple will imitate the way of the Lord. Those who are concerned with saving their lives, or gaining the world, will, on the contrary, forfeit life. Matthew's insertion of v. 27 suggests that he interprets this prospect of the gaining or forfeiting of "life" in terms of eschatological reward or punishment (cf. 13:41-43; 25:46).

The concluding saying (16:28; cf. 24:34) has been troubling to some readers, inasmuch as it incorrectly predicts the imminent Parousia of the Lord. Surely even Matthew's own readers would have recognized that the prediction had not come to pass. Elsewhere Matthew speaks of the delay of the Master's coming (e.g., 24:45-51). Perhaps in the present lection Matthew simply chose to overlook the detail of timing, convinced as he was that the Lord would, indeed, come again.

The lection offers rich possibilities for preaching. The awesome significance of our worshiping a suffering and crucified savior—a savior whose power was made manifest in weakness—often eludes modern Christians.

In part this is because time and familiarity with the accounts of the cru-cifixion have made us take Jesus' suffering for granted. In part it is because the horror and shame once evoked by crucifixion have disappeared along with the use of this form of punishment. But for first-century Jews—who expected the heavenly redeemer to be lordly and victorious—Jesus' message of his own imminent suffering would have been shocking.

This portion of the passage can also serve as a classic illustration of the wisdom and the sovereignty of God. God's plan for humankind often clashes with that which humans think best. God's sovereignty and wisdom cannot be contravened, either by Satan or by those persons who unwittingly serve the devil's ends.

Jesus' teachings about the implications of his own suffering for followers (vv. 24-26) deserve thoughtful attention by the preacher. No doubt each will have a diffferent idea of what the charge to "deny oneself and take up one's cross and follow Jesus" means in the context of everyday, twen-tieth-century life. What should unite even the most wide-ranging appli-cations of the teaching is the hard truth that the way of the Lord is not an easy one. It can lead to suffering and consequently to feelings of aban-donment. But the faithful must rest assured that God is present, even in the hardest times (see the above discussion of Jer. 15:15-21), and that whoever "loses life for Jesus' sake" will find it.

The Sixteenth Sunday after Pentecost

Lutheran	Roman Catholic	Episcopal	Common Lectionary
Ezek. 33:7–9	Ezek. 33:7–9	Ezek. 33:7–11	Exod. 19:16–24
Rom. 13:1–10	Rom. 13:8–10	Rom. 12:9–21	Rom. 13:1–10
Matt. 18:15–20	Matt. 18:15–20	Matt. 18:15–20	Matt. 18:15–20

FIRST LESSON: EZEKIEL 33:7-9

The vocation of the prophet is compared to that of a watchman (cf. Ezek. 3:16-21). The watchman is a sentry who looks out over the wall of the city and warns its inhabitants of approaching persons (see, e.g., 2 Sam. 18:24-27; 2 Kings 9:17-20). If enemies approach and the sentry does not warn the city, and if an inhabitant dies at the enemies' hand, then the sentry is held accountable for failing to carry out his duty. On the other hand, if the sentry gives adequate warning and someone dies nonetheless, the sentry is not responsible, for he has done what he was required to do. So also the prophet must warn the wicked that retribution will be made unless they repent of their wickedness. If the prophet fails to carry out this task of warning, then he shall be held responsible for the unrepentant death of the wicked. On the other hand, if the prophet gives warning and the wicked still refuse to turn from their evil ways, then the prophet shall not be held responsible. He has done what was required of him.

The literary context of this passage may be exegetically significant. The passage is closely similar to one in the opening part of the book (3:16-21). At that earlier point, the watchman analogy served to underscore the weight of responsiblity upon Ezekiel as he uttered oracles about the impending doom of the city of Jerusalem. In 33:21-22 (just after the present lection), the report that the city has actually fallen marks a turning point in the book. At the time of the announcement, the sentry has already given his warning, and death has come nonetheless. From here on, Ezekiel will offer oracles of salvation. Why has the watchman analogy been repeated just prior to this announcement of the city's fall? Perhaps the reason is to make the point that, despite the disaster, the people's basic condition has not changed. They have lost their city, but they are not thereby exonerated. They still need to repent of their wickedness, lest even greater disaster come upon them.

The passage is significant because of its implication that persons can be held accountable for the moral state of others. (In this lection such responsibility is assigned to the prophet alone rather than to the people as a whole, but the corresponding lection from Matthew assigns responsibility to the church.) Lest the burden of such responsibility seem too onerous, God informs the prophet that the one who warns the unrighteous but gets no response will have satisfied the divine requirement just the same.

ALTERNATIVE FIRST LESSON: EXODUS 19:16-24

The period of solemn consecration described in 19:14-15 has prepared the people for the momentous occasion that now unfolds. The thunder and lightning and the blast of a trumpet (v. 16) portend Yahweh's own imminent descent upon the mountain in fire (vv. 18, 20). The people are terrified by the events, but Moses calmly carries out his role as God's chosen mediator. Verse 19 dramatically describes God's own confirmation of Moses' role (cf. v. 9): Moses speaks to God, and God answers him in thunder. Verses 20-25 describe God's instructions that Moses give additional warning to the people not to break through the barriers around the mountain to try to gaze upon God. The section may seem to be redundant—indeed, Moses himself thinks so (v. 23)! But the instructions serve to emphasize the terrifying holiness of God, a holiness so great that extraordinary measures are required of those who would encounter it. Thus far God has spoken only to Moses, but momentarily the people too will be addressed directly, and they must be prepared for the awesome exchange. The message of God's holiness reminds us that we are not to take our relationship with God for granted. God is indeed gracious and loving, and we do have unparalleled access to God through Jesus. Still, for Christians today as for the Hebrews on Sinai, God's holiness and justice call for the most profound humility and reverence.

EPISTLE: ROMANS 13:1-10

In this passage Paul imparts to the Romans practical advice for living the Christian life. The passage comprises two logically distinct sections. The first section treats Christian behavior vis-à-vis the state (vv. 1-7); the second treats behavior vis-à-vis one another (vv. 8-10).

In vv. 1-2 Paul declares that God is sovereign over the governing authorities (cf. Prov. 8:15-16; Wisd. of Sol. 6:1-3). Such authorities carry out God's will (though often without knowledge that they do so); therefore, Christians must obey them or else they will be opposing God's will and accordingly will bring judgment upon themselves. Paul insists that there is no need to fear the authorities, for, as executors of God's will, they punish only wrong conduct. By contrast, good conduct will receive the authorities' approval (vv. 3-4; here Paul presupposes a government that acts according to moral principles, and that therefore does indeed uphold the "God of order"). In vv. 5-7 Paul claims that obedience to the state is to include the payment of taxes as well as of the respect that leaders are due. In other words, believers must take their civic obligations seriously. Evil and fleeting as this world may be, one cannot disregard its demands entirely!

Clearly the teaching in 13:1-7 is subject to serious limitations, inasmuch as Paul's presupposition that the government will uphold moral principles— rewarding good and punishing evil—is not always valid. Governments often act in quite the opposite manner, rewarding evil conduct rather than good, and carrying out policies that run contrary to God's will for humanity. When such is the case, the validity of the entire teaching is called into question. Fortunately, Rom. 13:1-7 and the very similar 1 Pet. 2:13-17 do not make up the entire New Testament witness on the matter of Christian behavior toward the state. Taking a radically different perspective, the author of the book of Revelation insisted that the Roman government was promoting idolatry, which in any age is clearly opposed to God's will. The state is portrayed by the prophet John as the servant, not of God, but of Satan and the forces of chaos. Hence the author felt justified in calling his readers to passive but staunch resistance of the state (see esp. Rev. 13:1-18; 17:1—19:10). To refuse to meet the state's demands is understood in Revelation to be Christian duty. God will judge the idolatrous state (cf. Wisd. of Sol. 6:4-11) and condemn those who by obeying it have failed to walk according to the purpose of God.

The passage is a difficult one to preach. In some congregations hearers will no doubt resist the message that God works through the human structures and institutions of the state; in other congregations the message may be embraced too heartily and perhaps used as a defense for nationalism and controversial government policies. In both congregational contexts it would be helpful and prudent to tune an ear not only to Paul's message but also to traditions in the canon that express a different opinion on the subject.

Shifting gears, in vv. 8-10 Paul writes that love is the fulfillment of the law (cf. Lev. 19:18; Mark 12:31b and parallels). Christians "owe" one another a debt of love but otherwise should owe nothing to anyone. By "anyone" Paul probably means anyone outside the Christian community. Paul pictures a community whose members love and respect one another and support one another financially. As Paul had stated in 1 Thess. 4:9-12, such mutual love and financial independence from outsiders will surely command the respect of the latter. Today also, the love and mutual support of Christians for one another can be a strong testimony to outsiders of God's own love for humanity.

GOSPEL: MATTHEW 18:15-20

The preacher should approach this passage with care! Matthew's description of the procedure for discipline of offenders within the church contains a very harsh saying of Jesus (v. 17). Moreover, the passage as a whole has caused immeasurable pain through the ages, applied too often by the self-righteous who, in seeking to eliminate evil from their midst, succeed only in pulling up the wheat with the tares. Matthew himself seems to have recognized that the tradition harbored power for ill as well as good: he has counterbalanced it by bracketing it on the front end with the teaching that God desires not to lose any of those who go astray, and on the other end with Jesus' exhortation to forgive one's brother or sister "seventy-seven times" (or "seventy times seven"; i.e., an unlimited number of times).

The social historical setting which gave rise to the passage was very likely that of the church in the generations after Jesus' earthly ministry. The notion that Christians should admonish and exhort one another in their moral sojourn is by no means unique to Matthew; for example, see also 1 Thess. 5:12-14 and Gal. 6:1. Christians are ultimately accountable to God, but the New Testament writers are firm in their insistence that during this earthly life Christians are also accountable to each other. "Mutual admonition" is quite appropriate, though it is always to be carried out in a spirit of love and gentleness.

Matthew has Jesus insist that when a specific wrong has been committed, every effort be made to correct the offender with the least possible publicity and embarrassment (vv. 15-16; on v. 16 cf. Deut. 19:15). But if the sin is blatant and the sinner stubbornly unrepentant, then excommunication is deemed to be the only answer (cf. 1 Cor. 5:9-13; Titus 3:10). The church's decision in the matter will be binding also in heaven (Matt. 18:18; see also the above discussion of 16:19). Indeed, Christians can know that when they are assembled to carry out a disciplinary decision, they do so under the authority of Christ, who is present in the midst of their assembly (18:20; cf. 1 Cor. 5:4).

The passage about discipline can still speak to the church today, provided that we recognize its seriousness about the actions outlined therein. The preacher may choose to tie in the text from Ezekiel (33:7-9; discussed above). The emphasis in our society on individualism tends to foster the notion that we are in no way accountable to one another: There is no need for sinners to justify their actions, provided that they hurt no one; by the same token, there is no need for others to call them to account. But this lesson from Matthew teaches that in the church it will be different. Actions on earth have eternal consequences, and so believers may not stand idly by while their Christian brothers and sisters stray from the path of righteousness.

The statement attributed to Jesus in 18:17, that the unrepentant offender "shall be to you as a Gentile and a tax collector," is hard to fathom. Though

Matthew elsewhere transmits traditions critical of the Gentiles (e.g., 5:47; 6:7, 32), he also knows of positive traditions (e.g., 12:18, 21). And evidence overwhelmingly suggests that Jesus insisted on the acceptance of tax collectors, whose number included Matthew himself (10:3)! The saying at 18:17 has its origin in a situation of controversy and tension; it has surely outlived its usefulness to the church.

The assurance of v. 20, that Jesus is present wherever two or three gather in his name, is one of the most beloved passages of Scripture. Some readers may initially be disturbed to discover that Matthew applies the promise to the situation of church discipline. In other words, the evangelist seems to be saying that Jesus' promise of his own presence applies specifically whenever two or three members of the church go to reprove a Christian brother or sister (18:16), or even to cast that person out of the church (18:17). On those occasions Jesus will be present to confer his authoritative approval (cf. 1 Cor. 5:4, where Paul insists that his own spirit and the Lord's power will be present when the Corinthians discipline a moral offender). Is it reasonable to loose the saying in Matt. 18:20 from this envisioned context of church discipline, as believers have so often done? In other words, can we be confident that Christ is indeed in our midst whenever we gather in his name, whether to worship, to work, or to enjoy Christian fellowship with one another? Certainly the answer is ''yes!'' For as Matthew elsewhere reports, Jesus has promised to be with us always, to the close of the age (28:20).

The Seventeenth Sunday after Pentecost

Lutheran	Roman Catholic	Episcopal	Common Lectionary
Gen. 50:15–21	Sir. 27:30—28:7	Sir. 27:30—28:7	Exod. 20:1–20
Rom. 14:5–9	Rom. 14:7–9	Rom. 14:5–12	Rom. 14:5–12
Matt. 18:21–35	Matt. 18:21–35	Matt. 18:21–35	Matt. 18:21–35

FIRST LESSON: GENESIS 50:15-21

Jacob (Israel) has just died, and now Joseph's brothers are fearful that Joseph will finally take revenge upon them for having sold him into slavery when he was a youth. He had forgiven them (see 45:5-8), but apparently they worried that their father's death would revive Joseph's hard feelings. So they come to him and relate to him an apparently fictitious appeal by Jacob that Joseph forgive the brothers. Joseph weeps at the appeal (50:17; cf. 45:2, 14-15). He reiterates his faith in divine providence, concluding that the brothers' evil act of selling him into slavery years earlier had been part of God's larger plan to keep many persons alive (50:20; cf. 45:5-8). Only because Joseph had come as a slave into Egypt had he been able successfully to guide that country—and indeed the whole world—through the long famine. Again Joseph forgives the earlier treachery of the brothers. His forgiveness of them and his faith in God's providence are inseparably related.

The offense committed by Joseph's brothers years ago was horrifying: Out of petty jealousy they had sold their own brother into slavery. No wonder they feared that he would now, at long last, take revenge upon them! One can imagine their fear at this prospect of punishment had been gnawing at them ever since their reunion with Joseph. But Joseph did not bear a grudge; on the contrary, he forgave willingly, completely, his love for his brothers pouring out in a stream of tears. His willingness to forgive enabled him even to see the good that had come about as an indirect result of his brothers' actions. The account of Joseph's generosity in forgiving his brothers could be used with great effect to illustrate and amplify the Gospel lesson (discussed below).

ALTERNATIVE FIRST LESSON: EXODUS 20:1-20

Here God spells out the demands of the covenant to which the people had in principle assented earlier (Exod. 19:8). The present ordering of the narrative suggests that the "ten commandments" (Hebrew: "ten words," so called on the basis of Deut. 4:13; 10:4) are the only part of the covenant demands that were spoken directly to the people by God. In 20:19 the people request that Moses once again act as mediator for them, so overwhelmed are they by the experience of God's presence.

The commandments themselves are in the form of "apodictic" prohibitions (absolute prohibitions, as opposed to the "casuistic" or conditional laws of 21:2—22:17). 20:2 is a preamble, in which the people are reminded of what God has done for them, and therefore of the claim that God has upon them (cf. 19:4-6). The actual commandments follow. The first four pertain to the people's relationship to Yahweh; the last six pertain to their relationship to one another and will help to regulate community life in the promised land.

The change in the people's reaction to Yahweh's theophany is significant. When Yahweh had first offered to establish a covenant relationship with them, they answered as with a single voice (19:8). But the confidence that seems to be implied by that earlier unitary response diminishes as a result of their encounter with the living God. Hearing God speak first to Moses (in thunder; 19:19) and then directly to themselves in the giving of the Ten Commandments caused the people to tremble with fear (20:18). The "fear" of God is the acute awareness of God's holiness and majesty, against which all human striving seems petty and sinful (cf. Isaiah's reaction to an encounter with God in Isa. 6:5; or Peter's reaction to Jesus in Luke 5:8). Moses assures the Hebrews that it is a good thing to have such fear before their eyes, that they may not sin (20:20). But Moses tells them also that (provided they stay within the limits set for them by God in 19:21-25) they need not "fear" that God will strike them down, for God is not capricious or willfully destructive.

This is a difficult passage to preach, in part because it says so much. One could easily devote an entire sermon to each of the commandments. For preachers who wish to remain with the lectionary and treat the passage in a single Sunday, one approach would be to focus on the significance of God's choice to enter into a covenant relationship with Israel. God made a commitment to the people and in return expected lives which were lived in obedience to God's desires. The Sinai covenant did not come without strings attached: God has delivered the people in the past and will do so in the future, but God's act of commitment affects the way persons are to live their lives on earth.

EPISTLE: ROMANS 14:5-12

Here Paul gives practical advice on achieving communal harmony when strong differences of opinion exist about the proper way to live out one's religious calling. Paul generalizes from principles forged in pastoring the fractured community at Corinth. In 1 Corinthians the discussion had concerned the specific issue of whether or not it was permissible for Christians to eat meat that had been sacrificed on the altar of an idol (1 Corinthians 8, 10). In Romans the issues seem to be more general: whether or not to practice ascetic self-denial, forgoing meat and perhaps also wine (14:2; cf. v. 21); and whether or not to observe certain days as holy (e.g., the Sabbath, Jewish feast days, perhaps days designated as auspicious by pagan astral speculation; cf. Gal. 4:8-10; Col. 2:16). Paul seems deliberately to be making his advice general. He has never visited the Roman church and so doesn't know the situation firsthand—but he knows the *kinds* of disputes that almost inevitably arise when persons of very different backgrounds try to live in community. One may generalize his teachings even further to make them applicable to the present situation of the church. Today also, Christians may have disagreements about how to live the Christian life. Among those who attempt to resolve such disagreements, the goal of assisting others in their walk of faith and of building up the church should be paramount.

In vv. 1-4 Paul has sketched out the different opinions about food consumption and has asked rhetorically what right Christians have to judge the servant of "another" (i.e., of God). It is before their own masters that the servant will "stand" (i.e., be vindicated) or "fall" (i.e., be judged guilty). (Paul will come back to the theme of judgment in vv. 10-12.) In v. 5 Paul sketches out the range of opinions about whether or not to observe holy days, advising that the Roman Christians "let everyone be fully convinced." In other words, it is more important that believers act in harmony with their moral convictions than that they adopt a particular behavior (cf. 14b; 22b-23). If each one is fully convinced that what he or she is doing is right, then the action—whatever path is chosen—will serve to honor the Lord (vv. 6-9). Paul's basis for this statement is his certainty that as Christians the members of the church in Rome are not living for themselves, but for the Lord (v. 7a; the clause should be introduced by "for" or "because"). Hence if they are acting in good conscience the Lord will consider their action acceptable.

The text would have had several effects upon the Roman church. To begin with, it would have deterred people from judging others based on the forms of their religious behavior: Done in good conscience, all behavior is acceptable to God. (Of course Paul takes for granted that some limits still obtain; e.g., one cannot kill another person in good conscience and call it acceptable to God!) This deterrence of judgment would in turn have enabled the community to become more united. Another effect of the passage would have been to give confidence to individuals who were uncertain about whether their own actions were pleasing to God. Paul declares that, provided such persons have examined their works and have become "fully convinced," then their behavior will be regarded not only as acceptable but also as *honoring* God. These effects of Paul's teaching would be equally relevant in the church today.

In vv. 10-12 Paul comes back to the theme of judgment. The recognition that each of us will be judged by God causes us to hesitate before judging each other (compare 1 Cor. 4:3-5, where Paul declares that he is at peace even when others are judging him, for he knows that it is only the Lord's judgment that matters). Rather than judging one another, Christians should "pursue what makes for peace and mutual upbuilding." They should look to the interests of others rather than only to their own interests. This might require that they willingly forgo the consumption of a particular food or drink if it means the salvation of a brother or sister (vv. 13-23; cf. Phil. 2:1-13, discussed below). The most important thing is that persons act in accordance with their own consciences, "acting from faith."

GOSPEL: MATTHEW 18:21-35

This lection continues the discussion of relations within the Christian community begun in 18:15, and provides a welcome balance to the preceding passage on admonition and excommunication. Indeed it seems likely that Matthew intended for vv. 21-35 to remind readers of what is the proper attitude for those who carry out the discipline described in vv. 15-20. Peter asks how often he ought to forgive a (Christian) brother or sister who sins against him. The answer "as many as seven?" that he himself proffers would have been regarded as generous by many. But Jesus counters that one must rather forgive *seventy-seven* times (many translations read "seventy times seven"). Perhaps the figure is intended to be a counterexample to Gen. 4:24; in any case it is not to be taken literally. Jesus' point is that one must be exceptionally generous in forgiving others.

This point is illustrated by the ensuing parable. The king in the parable represents God, who also will one day "settle accounts with his servants" (v. 23; note that in 25:31-34 the Son of man is referred to as "the king"). The size of the debt from which the king released the servant (10,000 talents) was staggering; a single talent was more than fifteen years' worth of wages for a laborer! The amount seems deliberately exaggerated, as if to underscore the extravagance of God's own forgiveness of human sinners. The servants in the story represent Christian brothers and sisters, who similarly watch out for one another (v. 31). Otherwise the details of the story should not be pressed. Its main point is clear enough: Because the Lord has forgiven Christians for their many sins, they likewise ought to extend forgiveness to one another (cf. 6:12, 14-15). The concluding warning that God, like the king, will deliver unforgiving Christians "to the torturers" (RSV: "jailers") is consistent with the Gospel's picture of severe punishment for the unrighteous (see , e.g., 8:12; 13:42, 50; 22:13; 24:51; 25:30). Still, many readers find that the divine vindictiveness expressed here does little to promote a genuine spirit of forgiveness. The preacher may well choose to focus in more positive terms on the call to be generous in forgiving others. The story about Joseph's forgiveness of his brothers in Gen. 50:15-21 (discussed above) could serve as a positive and powerful illustration of human forgiveness.

To be generous in forgiving others need not imply that one has no ethical expectations. Quite the contrary: Matthew's Gospel strongly emphasizes that Christians are expected to meet the highest possible moral standards. They must strive to achieve the higher righteousness (5:20) and will be held accountable for their deeds at the judgment. At the same time, when they are in community with one another, they are to be liberal, even extravagant, in their willingness to forgive "from the heart" those who offend them. To refuse to do so would be to mock the inestimably greater generosity of God, who has first forgiven us.

In the simple world of the parable, actions and obligations are clear-cut. The amount owed is indisputable, as is the king's generosity in forgiving the debt. In the face of such great mercy, it seems astonishing that the servant should be unwilling to extend mercy to another. But in real life, matters are not so self-evident. Therefore, in a sermon on this passage, the preacher may want to begin with the news of God's grace and forgiveness: God forgives our sins, overlooks our shortcomings, and recreates us in Christ Jesus. Only when we begin to perceive God's remarkable love toward us are we filled with the desire to share that love with others. Next the preacher could discuss forgiveness as the ultimate expression of such love. Christians are called to forgive those who have wronged them, and (equally important) to tell the Good News wherever there is a need for God's grace and mercy in our broken world. It could be pointed out that "forgiveness" implies neither that one condones the action in question, nor that one will continue to overlook a chronic problem. The call to forgiveness means, rather, that believers must emulate the grace of Christ, who loved his enemies even as he tried to save them from their evil ways. Recall that Jesus expressed forgiveness of his enemies even in his darkest moment—as he hung upon the cross (Luke 23:24).

The Eighteenth Sunday after Pentecost

Lutheran	Roman Catholic	Episcopal	Common Lectionary
Isa. 55:6–9	Isa. 55:6–9	Jon. 3:10—4:11	Exod. 32:1–14
Phil. 1:1–5, 19–27	Phil. 1:20c–24, 27a	Phil. 1:21–27	Phil. 1:21–27
Matt. 20:1–16	Matt. 20:1–16	Matt. 20:1–16	Matt. 20:1–16

FIRST LESSON: ISAIAH 55:6-9

The present lection continues the divine summons of Isa. 55:1-3 (a lection for the Eleventh Sunday after Pentecost, treated above). But now the invitation to come to the Lord is seen to carry with it an imperative: The wicked are to forsake their ways, and the unrighteous to abandon their unrighteous thoughts. The Bible often portrays recognition of one's own sinfulness and the desire to repent as consequences of an encounter with the holy God (see the discussion of Exod. 20:1-20 above). Hence the prophet's invitation to come to God and the subsequent command to repent and reform are like two sides of one coin. The prophet proclaims that God will be merciful and pardon iniquities, thereby assuring that God acts "in good faith," out of a genuine desire to gather a recommitted people. But the hearer is not to presume on God's grace: It is *now* that the Lord is near and may be found (v. 6); the proper time for a response is not some indefinite date in the future, but "today, when you hear God's voice" (Heb. 3:7).

In vv. 8-9 God informs the people that the divine plan is far greater than they can see from their limited perspective. To the Israelites in Second Isaiah's audience, who were in exile in Babylon and who felt as though God had forsaken the promises to the patriarchs (see the discussion of Isa. 55:3-5 above), it must often have seemed as though God were not really in control of the events of their lives. In this regard they were in the same position as an earlier generation of Hebrews, who had doubted whether God could lead them out of bondage in Egypt. To persons who feel abandoned, or who have lost faith in God's providence, the invitation to "come to" God might seem less than compelling. But God extends the invitation nonetheless, and suggests that the hearers themselves need to repent. They may suppose that God is not in control, but the truth is that God's designs are beyond their limited comprehension (vv. 8-9; cf. Rom. 11:33-36). God's word is sure: Like the rain that brings forth seed to the sower, so shall God's word bear abundant fruit (vv. 12-13). The last two verses picture the Israelites' imminent redemption in terms of a new exodus. Just as the Lord had earlier answered the Israelites' "groaning" with release from bondage, so would God do now.

ALTERNATIVE FIRST LESSON: EXODUS 32:1-14

The themes of human sin and divine forgiveness run like bright threads through chaps. 32–34 of Exodus. Chapter 32 recounts the people's disobedience when Moses was on the mountain and the consequent annulling of the covenant. God will eventually forgive the people and renew the covenant (chap. 34), but only because Moses intercedes on the people's behalf (cf. Ps. 106:23) and because the Lord is merciful and gracious. The events described in today's lection—the story of the golden calves—demonstrate how utterly undeserving of such grace the people are. Their idolatrous worship of the calf is a far more serious transgression than the indifference to God's providential care exhibited by their earlier "murmuring." The new incident is nothing less than outright repudiation of their covenant relationship with God. Certain features of the biblical author's narration suggest that the incident was understood to epitomize Israel's entire subsequent history as a "stiffnecked" and idolatrous people.

In 32:1 the remark that the people "gathered themselves together against [RSV: "to"] Aaron" implies a degree of compulsion. Aaron cooperates by fashioning the calf, but his comment in v. 5 suggests that he understood the purpose of the idol differently than did the people: In Aaron's eyes, the calf would provide, not an alternate god, but simply a different vehicle for worshiping Yahweh (RSV: "the LORD"). Still, Aaron is not to be exonerated; he fashioned the calf with his own hands (v. 4) and later denied having done so (v. 24). The people's acclamation of the single golden calf as "the gods [plural] who led them out of Egypt" has suggested to many scholars that the biblical author is shaping the account to recall events described in 1 Kings 12:25-33. After Solomon's death, Jeroboam had instituted the worship of golden calves, proclaiming "Behold your gods, O Israel, who brought you up out of the land of Egypt" (1 Kings 12:28; cf. Exod. 32:4). By means of this allusion to the Jeroboam incident the author of the Exodus account commented unfavorably on the unacceptable style of worship in the Northern Kingdom during the author's and his readers' own day. In subsequent generations also, the incident with the golden calf would be used by Jews as the parade example of Israel's stubborn rejection of Yahweh and consequent worship of idols (cf. 1 Cor. 10:7).

At Exod. 32:7 the narrator's attention shifts to the top of the mountain. God repudiates any relationship with the people, saying to Moses that "*your* people, whom *you* brought up out of the land of Egypt" have corrupted themselves (v. 7; contrast v. 4b). God is ready to consume the sinful people in righteous wrath. But Moses beseeches God to "repent" of this intention, referring to "*thy* people, whom *thou* has brought forth out of the land of Egypt." By this subtle use of pronouns and also by more direct appeals (including recollection of the earlier covenant with the patriarchs), Moses persuades God not to destroy the people. It is worth noting that Moses never tries to excuse the people's action (contrast Aaron's words in 32:24), but instead appeals to God's prior commitment to the people. The remainder of the story tells of Moses' own anger upon encountering the people, his shattering of the tablets of the law (signifying the breaking of the covenant), and of God's selective punishment (rather than total destruction) of the people.

EPISTLE: PHILIPPIANS 1:21-27

In vv. 21-26 Paul concludes the reflection begun in Phil. 1:12 on his personal situation. He seeks to ease the Philippians' worries about him. In v. 12 he had rejoiced that, paradoxically, his imprisonment was serving to foster the proclamation of the gospel (vv. 12-18). He expects that his personal situation—even if it should lead to his death—will serve to magnify Christ (vv. 19-20). Verses 21-26, part of today's lection, elaborate this point.

The lection begins with Paul's claim that for him "to live is Christ, and to die is gain" (1:21). Clues to the meaning of this familiar but somewhat obscure sentence may be found later in the letter, in 3:7-14. In the time since Paul was called to be an apostle, Christ Jesus has "made Paul his own" (3:12; cf. 2 Cor. 5:17; Gal. 2:20); hence for Paul "to live is [to live for] Christ." Moreover, as an apostle Paul willingly suffered the loss of whatever "gain" he formerly had (3:7) and is now willing to suffer even the loss of life, "becoming like Christ in his death" (3:10). He is confident that the loss of such earthly "gain" means that he will one day "gain Christ." In other words, he will one day be found to be "in Christ," having a righteousness "which is through faith in Christ, the righteousness from God that depends on faith" (vv. 3:7-8). For Paul, then, "to die is [to] gain [Christ]." Whether he lives or dies, Christ is honored.

Paul's own desire is to depart and hence to gain Christ (1:23), but he recognizes that more of God's work would be accomplished by his continued life on earth. Life "in the flesh" (i.e., in his earthly body) would mean "fruitful labor" (v. 22) and would be advantageous for the Philippians. Therefore Paul is confident that he will indeed remain alive for a time, helping their progress and joy in the faith and causing them to give glory to Christ on account of Paul's coming safely to them again.

The lectionary division after v. 27 is artificial, since vv. 27-30 are a single sentence in the Greek. In these verses Paul considers the Philippians' own situation. In v. 27 he instructs them that, whether or not he is able to come to them again, he hopes to hear that they are leading lives worthy of Christ. They should "stand firm in one spirit, with one mind competing side by side for the faith of the gospel" (cf. 2:2). Here Paul may be trying to counteract certain tendencies toward division within the Philippian community (cf. 4:2-3). He exhorts them not to be frightened by whatever they may suffer at the hand of their opponents; resolute confidence on the Philippians' part will be on the one hand a sign of their own salvation, and on the other hand a sign of their opponents' demise. Paul feels certain that the Philippians are indeed destined to suffer for Christ's sake, just as Paul has suffered.

The preacher could focus on the example set by Paul, who is joyously confident in a situation that many would have found overwhelming. He is in prison and does not know whether he is to live or die. He calmly considers each of the options and declares himself willing—even eager—to face whichever path the Lord chooses for him. Paul's confidence stems from his absolute trust that his destiny is in the hands of a loving Lord. The preacher may find that the depth of Paul's repose in the face of crisis is difficult for many modern persons to comprehend. But then, perhaps it was impossible even for Paul to comprehend. He knows that God responds to human needs and grants peace to those who pray—but he describes this "peace of God" as something that "passes all understanding" (Phil. 4:4-7). The magnitude and incomprehensibility of God's peace can be experienced by all the faithful but cannot be explained in rational terms.

Paul's peaceful acceptance of his future must have had a calming and empowering effect on the Philippians—who, after all, knew him personally and surely worried about what would happen to him. His example would have inspired them—as it inspires believers today—to put aside fears for their own lives and to trust in the Lord. Certainly Paul wanted his words to have this inspiring effect: He exhorts the Philippians to take a stand beyond the reach of fear, firm in one spirit, striving together for the faith of the gospel (v. 27).

GOSPEL: MATTHEW 20:1-16

This parable is made difficult by the conclusion in v. 16, which does not match the point of the story in vv. 1-15. The gist of vv. 1-15 seems to be that God's love and grace are totally unmerited, as is the wage given to the workers hired last. An analogous story is found in Luke 15:25-32, where the elder son begrudges his father's unwarranted generosity to the younger "prodigal" son who has returned. On the other hand, the point of Matthew's conclusion to the parable of the workers in the vineyard is that "the last will be first, and the first last" (v. 16). Elsewhere this saying refers to the reversal of fortunes at the eschaton (see Matt. 19:30; Luke 13:30; cf. Luke 14:11), but the only "reversal" in the parable under study is the rather trivial matter of the order in which the workers are paid. It seems likely that Matthew has joined v. 16 to the parable in order to make it illustrate the preceding point about the reversal of fortunes that the disciples (and presumably also the members of Matthew's own church) will experience in God's kingdom (19:28-30).

Thus we can identify at least two meanings of the parable: the meaning that Jesus must originally have intended (20:1-15), and the meaning of the parable as Matthew has reinterpreted it (19:28-30; 20:16). Probably Jesus first spoke the parable in order to reprimand religious leaders who resented his proclamation that the outcast and sinners would be admitted into God's kingdom along with those traditionally regarded as "righteous." Luke provides such a setting for the story of the prodigal son (Luke 15:1-2), and it is reasonable to infer an analogous motive for the parable of the workers in the vineyard. Spoken in such a setting, the key elements of the parable would have been the householder's generosity to the ones hired last and the inappropriate resentment of the ones hired first. To persons who begrudge God's grace toward those who have not shared their strenuous efforts to live righteous lives, God proclaims, "I am doing you no wrong . . . or do you begrudge my generosity?" (Matt. 20:13-15; cf. Luke 15:31). On the other hand, as Matthew has reinterpreted the parable by the addition of v. 16, it teaches that those who are now "last" in the world's eyes because they have left everything to follow Jesus (cf. 19:27) will receive tremendous reward "in the new world." "For many that are first will be last, and the last first."

A sermon based on this passage could take several different shapes, depending on which elements of the parable one chooses to emphasize. The householder's generosity toward those hired last may inspire a sermon on God's gracious offer of forgiveness, even to those who find themselves at "the eleventh hour": It is never too late to repent and reform. (If choosing this route, the preacher may choose to tie in the lection from Isaiah 55, discussed above.) The words to the servants who resented the householder's generosity may serve as the basis for a reflection on God's desire that Christians accept the repentant into their midst without judgment or jealousy. Or, the final saying of the parable in its canonical form (20:16) may lead the preacher to reflect on God's promises that sacrifice and commitment in this life will not go unrewarded.

The Nineteenth Sunday after Pentecost

Lutheran	Roman Catholic	Episcopal	Common Lectionary
Ezek. 18:1–4, 25–32	Ezek. 18:25–28	Ezek. 18:1–4, 25–32	Exod. 33:12–23
Phil. 2:1–5	Phil. 2:1–11	Phil. 2:1–13	Phil. 2:1–13
Matt. 21:28–32	Matt. 21:28–32	Matt. 21:28–32	Matt. 21:28–32

FIRST LESSON: EZEKIEL 18:1-4, 25-32

Ezekiel quotes a proverb that must have been current among his contemporaries: "The fathers have eaten sour grapes, and the children's teeth are set on edge" (18:2; cf. Jer. 31:29). He notes that the people are applying the proverb to the land of Israel. Given the historical context (shortly after the first deportation to Babylon), the people's use of the proverb suggests that they interpreted their own exile to Babylon as divine punishment for the iniquity of their forebears. Ezekiel insists that such is not the case: God reckons to each person according to his or her own works. Children are not punished for the sins of their parents, nor vice versa. Hence the exile cannot be blamed on an earlier generation: The present inhabitants of Israel must take the responsibility upon themselves. This notion that God does not punish for the sins of persons over whom one has no control is not a new principle; see Deut. 24:16. The law in Deuteronomy was a countermeasure to the custom of punishing all members of the wrongdoer's family, even if the members were themselves guiltless (see, e.g., Josh. 7:24-25; cf. Exod. 20:5).

In vv. 5-18 (omitted by the lectionary) Ezekiel gives specific examples to illustrate his point. Verses 19-20 offer a summary, and vv. 21-24 extend the basic principle to cover the various periods within the life of an individual. The lection picks up again at v. 25, with Ezekiel's insistence that the people's objection to the prophetic message constitutes a failure to comprehend God's justice. The people accuse God of injustice, when it is they themselves who truly are unjust. Ezekiel's refusal to let the people pass the blame for their current condition onto their ancestors should have compelled them to take a hard look at themselves and to acknowledge their own iniquity. Verses 30-32 warn that unless they do so and repent, they shall surely die. To use the biblical idiom, if and when they do die, their blood shall be upon their own heads, for God desired that they repent. God takes no pleasure in death; hence it is God's desire that the people make a choice for life by repenting of their sin.

In some contexts Ezekiel's insistence that persons are not punished for the sins of others could offer comfort. If a person's own relatives had seriously offended God, then it would be important to hear that God punishes only the guilty parties. But the teaching cuts both ways, and in Ezekiel's own context it is not meant to offer solace. Rather, it is used to admonish the people for trying to blame others rather than themselves. The preacher may choose to treat the passage in conjunction with the lection from Matthew (21:28-32; discussed below), which similarly chastises persons for accusing others of sin when they themselves are guilty. Given human reluctance to acknowledge personal guilt or blameworthiness, the danger that we ourselves shall fall into the same practice as those addressed by Ezekiel is ever present.

ALTERNATIVE FIRST LESSON: EXODUS 33:12-23

Once again Moses must intercede with God on the people's behalf. Because of the breaking of the covenant (see the discussion of the previous lection from Exodus), God has determined not to accompany the people into the promised land. The stubborn and sinful people are so unfit to be in God's presence that, were God to accompany them personally, God's holiness would consume them (33:3, 5). God informs Moses that an angel— a kind of alter ego—will be sent to accompany them instead. In response to this information, Moses pleads with God, recalling once again God's earlier commitment to the people (vv. 12-13). Indeed, Moses argues, if

God does not personally accompany the people, then that which makes them distinct from all other peoples will no longer be in effect (vv. 15-16; the verses seem to be out of order, inasmuch as God has already granted the request in v. 14). Finally God relents (v. 17), but Moses seeks assurance: Having sought and been granted insight into "God's ways," Moses now seeks to behold God's glory. In v. 19 God agrees to meet this request, though divine sovereignty is also emphasized ("I will be gracious . . ."). Moses is allowed to see God's back as God passes by. But even Moses must be given protection in "the crevice of a rock" as God passes by, so holy and consuming is the glory of the Lord. The theophany to Moses is a prelude to the renewal of the covenant, just as the theophany to the people had been a prelude to the initial granting of that covenant (19:16-25, discussed above).

EPISTLE: PHILIPPIANS 2:1-13

Here Paul continues the exhortation to the Philippians begun in 1:27. All of his words in this passage are directed toward the goal of enabling the Philippians to become a stronger and more unified community of faith. Generally Paul seems to have been pleased with the Philippian church's state of affairs, but he may have worried that disagreements among certain members would eat at the fabric of the community (suggested by 4:2-3, where "Euodia and Syntyche" are persons who appear to be in conflict). But whether or not it was made in response to existing problems, Paul's exhortation to communal harmony in this passage provides an excellent foundation for a sermon on the same topic.

The string of conditional clauses in v. 1 do not reflect genuine doubt; Paul regards it as self-evident that there are indeed "encouragement in Christ, incentive of love, participation in the Spirit, and affection and sympathy." Hence the clauses serve to heighten the force of the imperative in v. 2: The Philippians should complete Paul's joy by living in perfect accord and like-mindedness. To achieve such a goal will require a sacrificial attitude on the part of each member of the community. They must humbly account others as better than themselves, looking to serve the others' interests and not only their own (cf. 1 Cor. 10:24, 33). As an example or model for them to emulate, Paul quotes a hymn about Christ Jesus, who willingly gave up his equality with God, humbling hismself by taking the form of a slave and becoming obedient unto death. God responded to this obedience by exalting Christ, transforming him from slave to the master ("Lord") of the heavens and earth, to whom all cosmic powers are subservient.

It is commonly thought that the hymn in vv. 6-11 is a piece of early Christian liturgical tradition, taken over by Paul and perhaps known to the Philippians already. Issues of authorship and background (the suffering servant of Second Isaiah? Jewish wisdom teachings? gnostic speculation?) are debated by scholars. For homiletical purposes Paul's *application* of the hymn is more important than are the debated issues.

Used in this literary context the hymn serves at least two purposes. First and most obviously, the hymn reinforces Paul's exhortation to the Philippians to look not to their own interests but to the interests of others, for such was the behavior of Christ. The Philippians are to be "servants" (literally "slaves") of others, as Christ was a servant, and as Paul and Timothy are servants (1:1). Paul was convinced that this ethic of servanthood would lead to the unity and upbuilding of the congregation. Today also, cultivating the sacrificial attitude that was counseled by Paul and modeled by Christ is essential if the church (both local and global) is truly to be the body of Christ in the world.

A second, more subtle purpose served by the passage is to suggest that if the Philippians follow Christ's self-giving example they will be rewarded, because the Christians' God is one who brings joy and glory out of suffering, life out of death (cf. Rom. 8:29-30 [discussed above]; 2 Cor. 1:9-10; 4:7-18). Just as God raised and glorified Christ, so will God raise and glorify the Philippians. (Note further that in 3:7-11 Paul cites his own life as a parallel to Christ's example and shares his hopeful anticipation that he, too, will be rewarded with resurrection from the dead.)

Paul's command in v. 12 to "work out [among yourselves] your own [plural] salvation" is yet another exhortation that the Philippian Christians strive to realize the goal of becoming a harmonious community united behind the common cause of serving Christ. In making this effort they will be backed with divine power, "for God is at work among you, both to will and to work" for God's good pleasure. By so living in unity, the Philippians will be a testimony to the world (v. 15), and a sacrificial offering to God on Paul's behalf, which will easily withstand divine scrutiny in the day of Christ (vv. 16-17; cf. 1 Cor. 4:13-15). Today also, a harmonious church community united in the cause of serving Christ is both a sure testimony to the world that Christ's spirit is active, and a fragrant and acceptable offering to God.

GOSPEL: MATTHEW 21:28-32

The parable, found only in Matthew, illustrates the evangelist's concern that Christians strive for "righteousness" by "doing" God's will (cf. 5:20; 7:21; 12:50; 25:37-40). The literary setting for the parable is one of controversy. Jesus has "stirred up" the city by his dramatic entry into Jerusalem

(21:1-11). Presumably his cleansing of the temple has aroused the ire of the religious leaders (vv. 12-13). And his refusal to disavow the messianic acclamation of the children has further enraged these leaders (vv. 14-17). They ask Jesus who has authorized him to do such things (v. 23; given recent events, it was a reasonable question). But Jesus outwits them by asking a counterquestion about John the Baptist: Was his authority from heaven, or from humans? The query is not an unrelated attempt to divert attention from himself: Jesus, like John the Baptist, is a prophet who has come to them "in the way of righteousness" (21:32). The religious leaders, who had not believed John and who do not now believe Jesus, recognize that no matter how they answer his question they will inflame the multitude.

The parable of the two sons is directed to these leaders. The second son said he would go but did not. Similarly, the religious authorities claim to do the will of God but in truth act otherwise by refusing to believe those who come to them in the way of righteousness. On the other hand, the first son said he would not go but afterwards repented and went. Similarly, for most of their lives the tax collectors and harlots (or, to generalize, the outcast and sinners) had failed to do God's will, but at the coming of John they repented and thus did God's will after all.

Considered in its literary context, the passage makes at least two points which are important for Christians to hear today. The first point is that appearances can be deceiving when one is trying to determine who is genuinely obedient to God. It may be that those whom society rejects (e.g., in Jesus' day, the "tax collectors and harlots") will ultimately be more in conformity with God's desires than society's upstanding citizens (e.g., the religious authorities). This finding should make us reluctant to pass judgment on the religious fidelity of other persons (cf. Matt. 7:1-5). A second, related point made by the passage pertains to the need for us to engage in critical self-reflection. The religious authorities were so busy passing judgment on Jesus and the outcasts who followed him that they failed to recognize their own disobedience to God. Like the second son, they claimed to do the Father's will, but by refusing to repent at the advent of John and then of Jesus, they failed to make good on that claim. So also today, the faithful should look first to themselves, lest in their preoccupation with judging others they themselves be found to fall short of God's desires for them.